B2B Street Fighting

Next Generation Business-to-Business Negotiation

By Brian J. Dietmeyer, President & CEO of Think! Inc.

Think! Inc.
business negotiation, redefined

Table of Contents

Foreword

My long-term colleague and partner, Brian Dietmeyer, is a master at taking leading edge ideas in the negotiation literature, developing them, and crafting them for the experienced negotiation professional. He combines the best that academia has to offer with real world expertise and a deep appreciation for the current competitive environment. His curiosity for ideas, and his vast experience as a former Marriott executive both shine through.

Business to Business Street Fighting is Brian's second book length contribution. This new work offers unique insights that are relevant as we enter the second decade of the new millennium. While I have had the opportunity to interact with and teach with many of the greatest negotiation scholars, Brian's perspective always provides me with new and very unique insight. I trust that his insights will also be useful for any experienced negotiation professional.

Max H. Bazerman
Straus Professor, Harvard Business School
Executive Committee, Harvard's Program on Negotiation

INTRODUCTION

Fight Back Against the Economic Meltdown

Make no mistake about it: we are in the middle of one of the most significant economic meltdowns since the Great Depression. As one senior executive of a Fortune 500 firm told me recently, "In the past, we've always waited for the market to come back, then we could resume. This one's not coming back. The market as we know it has changed forever." Since 2008, the sub-prime mortgage crisis, rising gas prices, the failure of major aspects of our financial systems, the evaporation of individuals' retirement savings, retirees being forced to go back to work, layoffs and massive government debt have all contributed, in the worst possible way, to a "perfect storm."

Nowhere is this change more evident than at the negotiating table. The meltdown has catalyzed buyers into an even more assertive, stubborn and frugal breed than in years past. In every deal you bid, buyers are demanding across-the-board price decreases and are more tenacious than ever about getting what they want; they know it's a buyer's market.

It's time to fight back. It's time for the street fighter in all of us to come out. It's time to redefine not only how we negotiate business-to-business deals but the nature of the deals themselves. Time to replace a long list of tactics, tricks, countermeasures, effective questioning and meditation prior to a negotiation with a ruthless approach based on facts and reality. And it's time to dispel, once and for all, the myths that get in the way of successful negotiation, and throw out the assumptions that keep you unprepared, confused and afraid that you don't know what will happen next.

To fight back, you'll need to know, at a level of detail not seen before, exactly what your company's value proposition is and how it fits each customer's needs better than the alternative – value that is not just a vague, esoteric, marketing-owned concept out of touch with street-level business negotiation. You'll need an effective, real-time process for leveraging that value one deal at a time so you can you maintain margins, competitive superiority and market share. If you don't, the next phase of this perfect storm will be nothing less than a free-for-all for profit margin.

If you're ready to spend the next two years getting your clock cleaned by reacting to buyers who demand across-the-board price decreases, leaving you no other option than to hand them all the negotiating power by default, by all means, put this book aside. On the other hand, if you want to fight back by preparing, predicting, and deflecting the negotiating punches that until now have kept you from winning at the negotiating table, then read on. I'll give you the skills to predict, prepare for and combat 97% of what today's market is currently dishing out.

The B2B Street Fighter: A Lean, Mean Negotiating Machine

When I think of a street fighter, two words come to mind: **lean** and **mean**. I envision two lean opponents, stripped of all the trappings – the ring, the gloves, the fans and the corporate sponsors – testing their wits, wills and stamina anytime, anywhere.

Many of you already think of negotiation as a street fight: a ruthless, blood-spitting, no-holds-barred scenario where you throw a series of random punches and counterpunches without really knowing what's going to happen next. But unlike the old-school notion of a bare-knuckled brawler bullying or throwing a sucker punch at his opposition, or even a couple of ruthless thugs going at it in some back alley, my modern-day street fighter is trained, disciplined and prepared for his challenge. He's more like today's ultimate fighter who knows his opponent, can anticipate any kind of attack – kick, punch, take-down or elbow throw – and has both offensive and defensive moves at the ready. If we, as B2B street fighters, come to the negotiating table prepared, have a plan and are willing to do what it takes to execute that plan – a series of strategic punches and counterpunches – negotiation will no longer be a simple free-for-all.

The world of sales negotiation training appears to share the view that negotiating is unpredictable. Consider the lists and scripts other books and training methodologies throw at you to supposedly help you practice your punches before the fight, titles like: *The 401 Things You Need to Know When They Say "No"* and *The 286 Tips That Will Guarantee Negotiating Success – Act Now And We'll Send You Our Bonus 342 Tips.*

But our lean B2B street fighter is in complete control and knows precisely what's going to happen. He leaves his gloves, his trainer, his mouthpiece and even the ring back at the gym and checks his mental baggage at the door. He doesn't use fancy footwork, smoke and mirrors, negotiating tips, tactics or tricks for verbal jousting, carefully planned scripts or buzzwords. He wins by being in charge of his faculties and being the most prepared. He concentrates on the fact-based data that gives him more control; assists in more rational decision making; prepares him to give better responses to the questions, arguments and pressure points that the other side may raise and; ultimately, helps him achieve better results. Our street fighter is confident and, in fact, courageous knowing that he can control the outcome of the negotiation.

> *Currently my nephew is staying in our home. As a fat-free, sculpted, ultimate fighter-in-training, he is no roughneck kid out to bully the next guy. He is a clean-cut, qualified and dedicated young man who is all about challenging himself to be the best. He eats with the religious zeal of a monk bending to his studies; everything is carefully weighed and calculated. He exercises constantly and is always ready for battle. To stay on top of his game, he takes Pilates, tae kwon do, Greco-Roman wrestling and boxing classes. He is strong in the cage because he works harder and earlier and is simply more disciplined than everyone else. To be lean, mean B2B street fighters, we need to do the same as my nephew: start earlier and be more disciplined than everyone else.*

And mean? Of course negotiating isn't about being ruthless, sneaky or cocky. But it is *all* about acquiring an unfair advantage: being more prepared than anyone else at the table to give customers what they really want, creating value for both sides and doing this long before anyone else is even thinking about it.

You're still probably thinking, "sure, but no matter how tuned and toned and prepared I get, in the end, I never know what's coming my way, and the conversation always comes back to price." Read on. I'm about to turn the inherent complexity of strategic B2B negotiation into a feature, instead of a liability, and show you how today's B2B street fighter can anticipate and prepare for 97% of what will happen in business negotiation. 97%!

Street Fighter's Credo

To get what he wants, our B2B street fighter must do three things:

- **His company:** He must fight for his company as its representative at the bargaining table and change the conversation from the price of his products and services to the value of his solutions.
- **His competitors:** He must fight against his competitors and their reactive instincts to behave irrationally and give away portions of their value proposition.
- **His customer:** He must negotiate with his customer to find the optimal solution to their business problem.

Just like the triumphant ultimate fighter who starts training long before a victorious beatdown, the B2B street fighter starts preparing for a negotiation well before he suits up and strides into the room with all those charts and graphs. This means being a lean, mean data-collecting machine: starting to gather data weeks, even months, in advance of the actual sit-down and using that data for a specific

---

B2B, B2C ... Isn't All Negotiating the Same?

In a word, no! The world tends to think of all negotiating as the same, but B2B negotiating is very different. It requires different skills than any B2C or B2C-like negotiating you may encounter in the course of day-to-day life.

One key difference between B2B and B2C deals is that B2B negotiations are very complex. They involve a lot of *moving parts* – information about the products, their value/benefits, the market, the competition, and the customer that come into play before, during and even after the negotiation is complete. Learning to use this data to our advantage ... that's why we're here.

purpose. Our street fighter is more geek than Goliath; his strength comes from the accumulation of well-documented data he can use to form rational, non-emotional responses when the time comes.

I can't emphasize enough the importance of starting data collection well before you get to the negotiating table. The earlier in the sales process you start, the easier it will be to catch people off guard because they're much freer with data. As you get closer and closer to negotiating a deal, they become more cautious and put on their poker faces. So if you start collecting data early, when the other guys are vulnerable, when it's all sunshine and giggles, the information flows naturally and freely.

At Think! Inc., our clients often say, "Thanks for rescuing us; your instruction really helped us out of a jam." But a successful negotiation strategy is not about being rescued two days before the negotiation, it's about preparing farther upstream by grabbing more data and building the courage you need to handle issues well before they appear. This is all part of being meaner: collecting and thinking about data and how to use it long before anyone else does.

And now you're thinking … "Data? What *is* all this data I'm collecting, where do I get it and how do I use it at the negotiating table?" Read on, my fellow negotiator, that is what this book is about.

So, B2B street fighters, do you want to learn how to come to the fight with confidence, knowing that you are ready to do battle under a variety of conditions in a multitude of settings against any number of highly trained, badass competitors? I offer you no scripts to follow, no secrets to memorize, no tips or tactics on which to rely. What I will teach is how to prepare, stay light on your feet, think fast and respond accordingly, and how to cut the fat and reduce the fight to the lowest common denominator: avoid a hit and hit back.

It's that simple.

CHAPTER

1

Negotiation Tactics Are 97% Predictable

Trends That Challenge Even the Best Negotiators

Think! Inc. recently conducted a study in conjunction with the Strategic Account Management Association (SAMA) titled *Negotiation for Sales Effectiveness: Benchmarking Current and Best Practice*. The study summarizes the current state of negotiations at hundreds of prominent Fortune 500 companies. (I refer to this study often throughout the book; it is reprinted in the Appendix for reference.) When combined with our many years of experience helping clients negotiate deals all over the world, the SAMA study has helped us identify the top five challenges faced by B2B negotiators and why the old-school approach just won't cut it anymore.

1. **More professional buyers:** 92% of respondents to the study reported facing a higher number of professional buyers such as procurement officers and senior sourcing executives during sales negotiations.

2. **Increasing price focus:** 91% reported increasingly price-conscious customers. (That's to be expected with the new breed of professional buyer.)

3. **More commoditization pressure (i.e., everything being sold is essentially the same):** 60% said deals are becoming more or somewhat commodity-like. With increasing pressure from professional buyers, we expect respondents to see even more commoditization pressure.

4. **Increasingly irrational competitive behavior:** As a response to buyer pressure, 80% said they see mounting irrational competitive behavior, such as competitors drastically lowering prices or giving away services. The lack of negotiation strategy drives irrational market behaviors and sparks price and giveaway wars, ultimately lowering margins for everyone.

5. **Fewer, longer-term, bigger and more complex deals (vs. a higher number of smaller, simpler, short-term deals):** 90% reported some kind of consolidation of their customer base.

The result is that deals are becoming bigger, more strategic and more important – for both sides. Here, negotiation plays a larger, more critical role because the relationship they negotiate is the relationship they live with.

So how can *B2B Street Fighting* help you address these five key issues?

More professional buyers ... are tough but predictable opponents. Let's face it – salespeople are good at selling. It's a skill that is both learned and taught, often to the exclusion of all else. In short, it's your core competence; it's what you do. Professional buyers, on the other hand, are good at negotiating. It's their core competence. Unfortunately for salespeople, negotiation training is often seen as a soft skills course, little more than a communications elective. As you have probably already discovered, negotiating with a professional buyer is different from selling to the businessperson for the account. *B2B Street Fighting* will show you how to face professional buyers without fear or intimidation by predicting and preparing for virtually every negotiating situation.

Increasing price focus ... becomes less important when you're selling value. Yes, many people, especially those sitting across from you at the bargaining table, are focused on price, but price is only one variable in any negotiation. *B2B Street Fighting* will help you learn how to increase the importance of your value proposition over and above any price discount your competitor is willing to offer and keep the conversation away from price.

More commoditization pressure ... but you're not selling "the same thing" as everyone else. When someone says, "Your product is the same as everybody else's," and "the other guy is cheaper," you need to know what value you can offer that no one else can. This book will help you learn to differentiate your solution from the competition's, offer more value for the dollar and clearly communicate that value to the customer.

Increasingly irrational competitive behavior ... is easily diffused with facts and preparation. Why do so many folks buckle under pressure in the final negotiation? The answer is a lot simpler than you might think: most have very little to no formal strategy for negotiation and no plan for where to go or how to get there. As a result, they approach negotiation solely on a deal-by-deal basis. Competitors (and you sometimes) are behaving irrationally because they don't have a solution to this problem. *B2B Street Fighting* will give you the tools to help you stay calm under pressure and keep your advantage even while others are giving stuff away.

Fewer, longer-term, bigger and more complex deals ... then make each one count. The homogenization of the modern corporate marketplace is taking a toll not only on how well, but also on how often you can use your street-fighting negotiation skills. For instance, where once there were Exxon and Mobil (two places to deal), now there is ExxonMobil (one place to deal). Fewer deals and bigger, more complex agreements complicate matters a lot.

Obviously, losing a good deal is bad, but fewer opportunities to negotiate a sale means living with a bad deal for a longer period of time. If you irrationally lose a deal, you may not have a chance to revisit or renew that contract for some time, so be careful of winning at any cost. By showing you how to break down deals on a case-by-case basis and look at them in context, rather than in a vacuum, *B2B Street Fighting* helps you ensure that both the short- and long-term consequences are considered during negotiation and create a win for both sides, no matter how big or long-term the deal may be.

Three Complex Problems, Three Powerful Counterpunches

In every negotiation, buyers use tactics to get what they want. My colleagues at Think! and I have studied the research (much of it conducted at our request), consulted all over the globe on live deals and put in thousands of hours at the bargaining table collecting and studying verbal negotiating tactics and looking for patterns. Here is just a small sample from our surveys of the thousands of verbal tactics that buyers have used to ask for concessions from sellers. See if you notice any recurring themes.

- Your price is too high
- What's the discount? What's the real price?
- I have no budget right now
- Your share requirements are too high
- Your amenity values are inflated
- Our goal is to cut our costs by 10% over the previous contract
- We have problems meeting the service-level agreements
- Our business model does not allow us to pay that type of premium
- This decision will be made based solely on price
- Lead times are long; let's lock-in prices, so we can stock your items and avoid lead times
- 10% off last price paid
- Lowest price wins
- And so on

By far one of the most compelling insights from our work has been this: Despite the prevailing belief that negotiating is "random and can't be predicted or planned for," the research clearly reveals that verbal negotiating tactics from all over the world follow very predictable patterns. When you look at the tactics buyers use to keep the seller reacting at negotiating table, 97% of them fall into just two categories:

- They reference an alternative to accepting what you offer: I will build it myself, I will buy from a competitor, etc.
- They leverage this alternative to bargain (that is, to ask for a concession) for something in return, such as a lower price, better terms, faster delivery, an extended warranty, additional products or services, etc.

Regardless of the exact words used, the message is loud and clear: "To me you're all the same, so if you want my business, I want something in return." Whether buyers go through both steps or straight for the concession, this behavior is present in as much as 97% of the negotiations we've encountered. By understanding what these 97% of buyers are doing during negotiation, we can begin to change the dynamics of negotiation. So what are they doing?

First, buyers approach the negotiation by treating your product or service as a commodity. Not necessarily stated as such, most verbal tactics clearly communicate that the buyer is approaching the negotiation as if all products are the same. Whether they really believe this is true or not, it effectively signals sellers to begin the battle for lowest price or most robust offer. We call this, applying **commoditization pressure**. Not surprisingly, increasing commoditization pressure was one of the five key trends reported by our SAMA study.

Tactic Process

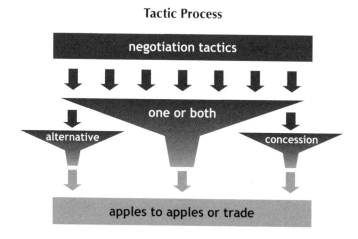

Next, whether they're bargaining for price or other concessions, buyers are constantly applying pressure to lower price or deliver more value for the price paid. Whether you're making an offer or you've already signed a contract, buyers are constantly applying **price pressure** to ensure they get both the best deal and the best price possible.

Now that we're wise to their tactics, it's time for a sound and simple negotiation strategy that changes the nature of the fight: one elegant, highly effective "counterpunch" for each punch the buyer dishes out.

1. To neutralize commoditization pressure, we'll reframe the negotiation into one in which it's clear that all products being sold *are not* the same. To do this, our first counterpunch,

15

consequence of no agreement (CNA) analysis helps you change the conversation about "alternatives" to an apples-to-apples comparison of what's really being sold.

2. To handle the never-ending price pressure, a second counter-punch, **trade analysis**, moves and keeps the focus away from price so you can have a more productive discussion about the value of what is being sold.

3. And finally, to keep you from reverting to a price-based nego-tiation after successfully selling value upstream, **the third counterpunch, multiple equal offers (MEOs)**, shows you how to tailor a deal that optimizes customer value – for the buyer and all of her internal customers – and gives you price premiums for the value you offer.

These counterpunches are not cute gimmicks, quick scripts or tactics you *memorize*. They are data-based analytical skills you *learn*; skills that work as well in your first negotiation as they do on your 101st. Based on experience gained during participation in 20,000 global deals, they are already the most effective, intuitive practices of *real people* doing *real deals* – we've just packaged them so they're leaner and meaner. So once you know, understand and master *B2B Street Fighting's* three counterpunches, you can control the uncontrollable, anticipate 97% of what's coming your way, and prepare fully to change the nature of the negotiation with your customers.

One Scary Little Sentence

Before we get started, I want to show how just knowing what buyers are up to can demystify even the scariest verbal tactics. Here's a daunting little sentence that, until now, you never wanted to hear at the negotiating table.

"I can get the same thing cheaper from someone else."

My clients hear this sentence or one just like it during almost every deal, typically at the *beginning* or very close to the beginning of the negotiation. For the unprepared, it is 10 short words that can really kick their butts. That's not surprising since most salespeople can't get past it; it's a negotiator's Achilles' heel.

No matter how many deals they've done, no matter how long they've been with the company, no matter how many times they've sat at that table, no matter how many times they've heard it before, each time is like the first: "I can get the same thing cheaper from someone else." Suddenly they're on the defensive, backpedaling to explain why this statement is wrong – and trust me, it is almost always wrong.

So how do you defend against this seemingly impossible statement? How do you counter such a far-reaching sentence? In the past you typically grabbed one of a dozen or more scripts you've tried to memorize, none of which adequately prepared you for this particular statement and its myriad interpretations. But now you know it is simply a common buyer tactic that attempts to commoditize what you're selling in order to create leverage to ask for something.

Using our new buyer-tactics decoder ring, let's take another look at those three distinct "punches" that our typical buyer is using to get what he wants.

- **"I can get the same thing"**: applying *commoditization pressure* to get you to play by their rules in a game where every product is the same.
- **"cheaper"**: Whether they want a lower price or more value for the price they pay, they are asking you for a concession.
- **"from someone else"**: a little reminder that there is always another seller ("alternative") waiting to deal if you won't give the buyer what she wants.

Before, during and even after you win the bid, rest assured the buyer will apply constant pressure to lower price, regardless of the value you negotiate or how hard you worked to sell value-creating solutions up until now. And we all know, whether early or late in the game, that when you negotiate commodity pricing of your products and services rather than total cost of ownership (TCO) for value-creating solutions, you lose revenue.

Now that you see what buyers are really saying, soon you'll be able to use your three counterpunches to fight back. But before we get started, I want to talk briefly about courage.

Data Will Help You Find Courage

What does your company really sell? Technically speaking, Ferrari sells cars. But the Ferrari *brand* is all about ego, luxury, money, status, cachet, etc. At Think! Inc. we offer workshops, white papers, seminars and conferences all centered around strategic business negotiation. But what we really sell is *courage*.

If the B2B street fighter is marked by any one skill, value or trait, it is courage. Courage colors every moment of a street fighter's waking life. It's not just how she acts under pressure; it's how she acts all day, every day, whether she's under the microscope or, more importantly, when no one is looking.

Some people may equate a title like *B2B Street Fighting* with cockiness rather than courage, but there is a difference. Courage is what makes deals happen the way the street fighter wants them to happen. Cockiness is an illusion, an attitude and a lie; it is acting out to make up for what a person lacks. Be forewarned: getting cocky is the surest way to lose a street fight, and it's no different at the bargaining table.

The goal of *B2B Street Fighting* is to give you the courage, the freedom, the skills and the data to make the right decisions at the bargaining table every time, regardless of the size, scope or scenario of the deal.

The data-collection and application skills you will learn here, and grow to covet, are part of a research-based process grounded in the way real people conduct real deals. They are based on reams of information about what the best-of-the-best do consistently. You can take heart that, once data is collected and analyzed for your customer/negotiation, you will be the strongest street fighter at the bargaining table exactly because of those geeky, analytic qualities.

Data isn't very sexy or glamorous, but when it comes to negotiation, it is the ultimate equalizer. Having data makes Davids out of Goliaths, and ignoring data makes Goliaths out of Davids.

Punch Lines:

Data isn't very sexy or glamorous, but when it comes to negotiation, it is the ultimate equalizer. Having data makes Davids out of Goliaths, and ignoring data makes Goliaths out of Davids.

CHAPTER

2

So What Are We Doing Wrong?

> *"The market has changed dramatically over the past 12 months. We have had limited exposure to negotiations in the past. Strategies are in their infancy, and training has been limited."*
>
> – Negotiation for Sales Effectiveness: Benchmarking Current and Best Practice

A client gave our company the greatest kudos the other day when he said, "You guys teach people to expect the unexpected." I thought for a minute and realized he was right. It made me think of a truism in the field of statistics: "Random events take on predictable patterns if you study them long enough – and closely enough." In other words, what looks like chaos to the uninitiated can be controlled, if you pay close enough attention for a long enough time to see the predictability of the randomness. The same can be said of the supposedly random, uncontrollable and runaway-street-fight nature of negotiation.

So what have we been doing wrong? What erroneous assumptions and behaviors have kept us from seeing these predictable patterns and taking action before? What decisions have our companies made, what methodologies have they adopted that are in fact *not* helping us win deals? And what prevailing myths about negotiation are overdue to be replaced with more current, productive thinking?

A Shocking Lack of Negotiation "Strategy"

Compounding the recent effects of global economic changes, changes at the street level are demanding a next-generation B2B negotiating methodology or, more accurately, a *formal* B2B negotiating methodology. I say this because after reviewing our extensive research and consulting on thousands of deals, I've discovered a shocking lack of negotiation strategy across the board – even in the most successful companies. In most cases, negotiation strategy is defined, by default, as aggregation of negotiation tactics. In contrast, the most successful negotiators use negotiation strategy to drive tactics.

I can already hear the wheels spinning in your head. "So if some companies are successful without a formal negotiation strategy then why do I need one?" What I didn't say is that they would *remain* successful, just that they'd somehow managed to be successful – so far – without one. This success can easily be derailed by just a few bad deals, by one very big, very bad deal or even by an economic meltdown like the one we're experiencing at the moment. Now more than ever the company without a firm negotiating strategy in place really is coming to a street fight with one hand tied behind its back.

Strategic Negotiation Is *Not* a Soft Skill

Does this quote from our SAMA research study sound familiar?

> *"We're in a rush (a 30-day mentality) to get the business, so we tend to give in to customer demands versus negotiating a win/win situation. Management is often too impatient to work through a negotiation process. They take the deal and move on, regardless of the fact that we're impacting future business dealings with the customer by demonstrating that we'll quickly and easily relent to their demands when put under pressure, especially if there is a danger of not securing the business in our time frame (i.e., quarter-end or year-end)."*

If you're like most of my clients, this scenario is indeed familiar. That's because for too long, negotiation has been considered a so-called soft skill, little more than tactics and verbal sparring that belong strictly in the domain of sales professionals. In fact, negotiation often takes a back seat to much more pressing sales issues such as forecasting, account management and opportunity management. But as we'll see, without negotiation everything mentioned above suffers, and with negotiation everything is improved.

So where do you fall? Do you think negotiation is a soft skill? Ask yourself:

- Do I have a consistent planning and execution process when it comes to negotiation?

- Do I give in to tough, last-minute demands out of fear of losing a deal?
- Do I assume the buyer always has more power?
- Do I spend enough time analyzing the customer's side of the deal?
- Do I get knocked back on my heels by tough verbal tactics?

If you answered yes to any of these questions, then you're in good company. Negotiation is vital to the lifeblood of each and every company doing business today. And strategic negotiation is neither a soft skill nor an elective; it is a comprehensive, analytical process that encompasses every department that touches sales. Well before any sales professional reaches the negotiation table, let alone makes that first sales call, there must be internal agreement on where the negotiation should go (strategy) and how sales professionals will get there (process). On a broader level, the strategy and process should be built around anticipating responses to key competitors and key customers.

Instead, the typical company leaves this to chance. They spend months writing a three-sentence mission statement for the company – one that few will people see and to which even fewer will adhere – then spend only a fraction of that time working on a strategic negotiation process that has a real impact on revenue and margin. This is a clear demonstration that the process of strategic sales negotiation is some combination of under-recognized, under-valued or simply not well understood.

My partner, Max, is fond of relating the story of a business-man at a cocktail party who brags about the amazing deal he just pulled off by playing some kind of old-school game and kicking someone's butt, usually making everyone in his audience feel less than confident in their own skills in the process. Max also points out that the rules of cocktail party conversation dictate that the businessman leave out the numerous deals he blew beforehand by being a jerk. After all, shooting from the hip can only take you so far. On the other hand, having a firm, set and published negotiation strategy in your company not only creates success at the bargaining table, but it also ensures continued success as long as the strategy is in place and is practiced consistently.

In fact, one problem we see with many traditional negotiation trainers is that even they incorrectly diagnose negotiation problems as random, unpredictable verbal tactics and therefore prescribe incorrect solutions (usually *more* verbal tactics). But from watching almost 20,000 business negotiations in 46 countries, we know that negotiation problems (and thus, their prescriptions) are more strategic than tactical and much more pattern-oriented than random. Good strategies drive good tactics and good strategies require data. Unfortunately, not enough companies invest in strategy before embracing the tactics.

Traps We Fall Into

> *Let us never negotiate out of fear. But let us never fear to negotiate.*
> – John F. Kennedy

Companies often come to me facing a major negotiation hurdle. Oftentimes, the hurdle is based on perception: they are intimidated by negotiation, they misdiagnose power or they freeze when they encounter a tactic for which they are unprepared. The problem is that when we're unprepared, we're much more likely to give in to perception versus reality. Let's look at some of the traps that are keeping us unprepared or ill-equipped to deal with our buyers' tactics.

We're Afraid

Regardless of how many different negotiation traps there are, they all have one thing in common: fear. Fear is a negotiation killer, no doubt about it. It shuts down your brain and rewires your thought processes. It makes you do things you normally don't do – and are likely to regret later. And fear makes your competitors behave in irrational ways that make it hard for you to predict or react to what they do.

What are some of the ways we exhibit fear in the negotiation process? You, your company and your team prepare to handle negotiation a certain way but when faced with the unexpected or a problem, you become reactionary and defensive rather than managing the negotiation. Your competence, confidence and clarity are broken, so you give away too much or settle for too little. Even a little fear is enough to tip the scales to the other side's advantage.

It's okay to feel fear, but it's not okay to let it cloud your emotions and trick you into responding differently than you would if you *were not* afraid. Fighters feel fear, then they get in the ring anyway. The B2B street fighter respects fear but controls it. How? By recognizing which negotiating traps are most likely to snare him and preparing for them.

We Don't Consider Both/All Sides

One of the deepest traps people fall into when facing a tough negotiation (and they're all tough, I realize) is not thinking enough about the other side (the competition). So, this is a good time to begin retraining your brain to see things from both perspectives, not just from your own. Preparing in a vacuum is not effective because negotiations don't occur in a vacuum. They are real-life events that take both sides into account and require real-time analysis and response. Yet no matter how prepared you are, you can and should expect the other side to do the converse of what you predict. Learning to negotiate on your feet, without relying on pat answers or templates, is the best preparation!

Other self-help guides *do* focus on the other side, but they don't go deep enough in their definition of who, exactly, is included. They define the *other side* as one person when, typically, there are multiple players involved, something we'll talk about later.

We Focus Too Much On Only One Part of a Deal

Another extremely common problem is allowing the negotiation to focus on one item at a time. Some negotiators tend to think very tactically, getting so caught up in one part of a deal that they ignore the others. They prepare for, do extensive analysis for, and guide the conversation around the parts they are most invested in or about which they're most concerned. When both sides come to the table with data that serves their purposes and defends their fiefdom, it becomes easy, and sometimes intentional, to lose track of the interrelationships of the parts of a deal for fear of losing the tactical advantage related to a specific part. And since no one on either side has all the data, often the big picture (and ironically, the path to achieving the most value for all) gets lost in the details.

Every deal is the sum of its parts, so it's important, even if *not* the source of a competitive advantage, to be prepared to discuss all parts of a deal.

We Make Only One Offer

A very common trap, one that surprisingly enough is even taught by some negotiating books, is that we make only one offer. What does this accomplish? Since deals always involve making multiple buying influencers happy, one offer most likely focuses on addressing the needs of only one buyer but not all of them. It communicates that you have assessed their situation and are now in the best position to tell them what they need most. And it immediately sets up a competitive atmosphere: if they disagree, they have what they need to shop around, whether for a better price or more features for the same price.

By shifting your perspective from simply offering one best-effort "deal" to a choice of deals that address different business relationships, you give customers choices they didn't know they would have from one seller. Each offer variation focuses on value and problem solving in slightly different ways, addressing the needs of different influencers in the customer organization and letting them choose what's most important.

We Undervalue Our "Value"

So if we know where and what most of the traps are, and we know they are fear driven, why do we keep reacting this way? To answer that, let me back up a little.

In the last chapter, I talked about two key tactics used by 97% of buyers – mention an alternative and leverage it to start the bargaining – and the three key problems this creates: commoditization pressure, price pressure and selling "value," then falling back to negotiating price. *Value* is a word we hear a lot these days. It's supposed to denote something worthwhile, significant, tangible and durable.

As modern-day salespeople, we are taught how to sell value. And, according to our research with SAMA, we are doing better at selling it more consistently. We recognize a customer's problem, work hard to find a solution and are trying to sell value upstream. But let's face it, most salespeople have a hard time selling value, in large part because they have only a vague idea of what it really is in a given deal. Sure, most marketing departments have formal value propositions, but true value in any given deal is simply a description of how one side can advance the customers business goals in a way the competition cannot. So on the back end of a deal, when our goals become cloudy, if we can't prove the value we tried to sell earlier, we default to negotiating price, undoing any positional or price advantage we'd gained up front. It's the classic bait and switch, except in this scam both sides lose. It's not intentional and, thankfully, it is preventable.

At Think! Inc., we teach that value actually shifts: from day to day, from deal to deal, from product to product and from company to company. As the customer looks at his alternatives and then at your proposal, value arises from the places where your solution meets his needs incrementally better. And this process of becoming a geeky street fighter teaches you to find, distill and absorb a whole new batch of research for any particular deal so you can find that value and meet this customer's needs in this deal.

In fact, value is invaluable because when you can prove it, you can often get a price premium. And shortly we'll learn how to **create true value** – value that customers will pay for – without sacrificing price or succumbing to the pressure to commoditize on the back end.

Sometimes The Opponent Is You!

Sometimes your company's approach to or attitude about negotiating actually works *against* you at the negotiating table.

Your Deals Tell the Market Who You Are

One impediment to negotiating success comes from a disconnect between account management and opportunity management processes. When properly integrated, these processes ensure that selling fundamentals (e.g., identification of key buying influences, the role played by buyers and value solutions for the client's business problems) are more consistently executed.

One of the major benefits of your company incorporating a more prescribed approach to negotiation into its selling framework is that it lets you strategically influence the marketplace. The deals your company makes communicate to the marketplace who you are as a company, so taking greater control of the negotiating process helps to ensure that the market will see your company the way you want it to be seen.

In the *Harvard Business Review* (November, 2004), Danny Ertel wrote, "I have found that companies rarely think systematically about their negotiating activities as a whole. Rather, they take a situational view, seeing each negotiation as a separate event, with its own goals, its own tactics, and its own measures of success." Further, he added, "that approach can produce good results in particular instances but it can turn out to be counterproductive when viewed from a higher, more strategic plane." In other words, organizations without a negotiation process and strategy are letting their tactics and deals present a picture of who they are in the marketplace by accident rather than by design.

On this front, companies appear to fall into two camps: either the negotiation constraints are so tight that the sales force is not empowered to make decisions, or the parameters are so broad that the market decisions they do make are inconsistent. Aligning negotiation strategy and process allows for centralized planning (strategy) and decentralized execution (process), thereby enabling those closest to the customer to make faster and more effective negotiation decisions while ensuring that companies can present themselves as they want to be presented.

Are You Learning From Your Past Successes and Mistakes?

Another significant benefit of negotiation alignment is that it facilitates organizational learning. We are constantly surprised by the inability of the most efficient organizations we work with to acquire central knowledge about the most common negotiation demands made by customers and by the typical gaps in competitive analysis when they attempt to sell a specific product to a specific customer against a specific competitor. Collecting, organizing and using such information can greatly benefit these organizations, in fact any company, by preparing them to counter anecdotal buyer claims or irrational competitive behavior in future negotiations. Specifically, as companies begin to implement a negotiation process they build *organizational memory* – a database populated with the key elements gathered and learned while negotiating – allowing them to begin to behave more effectively and consistently, thus improving and adding to the bottom line.

Negotiators Are *Not* Unpredictable Drunks

A pervasive belief about negotiation is that you can't plan for it and can't control it because nothing is predictable; negotiation is all reaction and no amount of proactive preparation will matter. The essence of this problem was poignantly captured in an offhand comment made by the editor of *Selling Power* magazine, a magazine we love and with which we have a good working relationship.

> *One day we were talking with one of the editors about having a more consistent and rational approach to negotiation – a strategy versus a moving target. The editor stopped us and said, "How can you do that? I mean, aren't all negotiators like drunks?"*
>
> *I asked her what she meant and she explained, "You know, you never know what they're gonna do."*

This comment does a good job of summarizing how a lot of us confront negotiation. We assume there's no way to know what the other side is going to do, which colors the way we try to deal with them. We treat negotiation like a moving target (like our editor's unpredictable drunk), so why even bother. We stop trying to predict the unpredictable and avoid the unavoidable.

> *Another case in point: I was speaking at a conference for the International Association of Contract and Commercial Managers (IACCM) recently, and the event was really illuminating. This was a room filled with truly world-class negotiators, so my team and I asked them the burning question that has*

preoccupied our office: "What is your biggest frustration about negotiation?"

The consensus was thus: "You can't really get your arms around negotiation; you never know what's going to happen from one minute to the next." In other words: negotiation is uncontrollable, so why are we talking about controlling it?

Indeed, feedback from this and other IACCM conferences is a variation on this same theme:

1. I'm in firefighting mode from the minute I sit down at the bargaining table. I'm getting slammed. I'm moving so fast I can't control it.
2. It doesn't matter what I do anyway because all these deals are "moving targets," so the best I can do is just try to keep up and do damage control.

Does one – or both – of these scenarios sound eerily familiar to you? I know they must, because these sentiments are echoed by the majority of our clients who come to us seeking relief – that is, quick answers for complex problems.

Only a few companies have a firm plan in place for negotiation. In fact, the "planning is futile" mindset is so pervasive that you are probably skeptical right now. You probably think there is no way you could you ever walk up to the bargaining table *without* your treasured lists and tips, your scripts and personality analyses. But you can. And you probably don't believe that I've used the three research-based counterpunches presented in this book to help hundreds of clients in Fortune 500 companies all over the globe close more than 20,000 deals. But I have.

Yours Is *Not* the Only Farm Being Given Away

Our recent SAMA study (see Appendix) benchmarked the current state of negotiation against other professional skills and practices in the selling and account management fields. Many of the respondents provided valuable quotes that I found both disturbing and enlightening.

When asked to describe the current state of negotiation at his or her company, one respondent explained, "We are giving a whole lot of value [away] for free because of the threat to lose what we've got right now."

Another said: "We allow situations to become explosive before we react. By the time we begin to address the issue, it is seldom viable to resolve."

And finally, this: "Because we continue to see prices erode, which tells me that part of our problem is in negotiating, we tend to either concede way too much and end up with a one-sided contract, or we fail to concede enough and lose the opportunity."

The range and familiarity of the quotes proved that not only are many companies working without a consistent and driving philosophy of negotiation but they are also offering scattershot solutions to what is basically a constant. In short, lacking the right data and reacting with **panic**, loss of **power** or **paralysis** is irrational, and it obliterates any opportunity companies might have to effect a successful negotiation.

At Think! Inc., we know – from our benchmarking research and our work around the world – that you really *can* learn to anticipate about 97% of what's coming your way, to expect the unexpected and to control the uncontrollable. But you must be open to a new solution that isn't 135 tips, tricks, etc., to cover every potential situation. And, in turn, I will redefine the prevailing notion of negotiation for you so you are more likely to be open to accepting our premise.

So here's the good news. You *can* control your fear. You *can* predict how a negotiation will turn out. You can respond to unanticipated or surprise tactics spontaneously and powerfully. You can begin treating value as *valuable* and stop sacrificing it the minute the negotiation heats up. You can master the three problems you'll face at the table – commoditization pressure, price focus, and selling value-creating solutions then negotiating price – by understanding and responding to them maturely and rationally with our three counterpunches. But here's the bad news: you really need to know them at the *black belt level*.

Have you ever heard someone brag, "My knowledge runs an inch deep but a mile wide?" This is basically someone confessing to being a know-it-all; they're admitting to knowing very little about a whole lot. The B2B street fighter doesn't claim to be a know-it-all; he knows three things very, very well, and those three things inform his every win at the bargaining table.

By now, I hope the need for a formalized negotiating strategy is clear. A ton of books have been written on negotiation by self-proclaimed experts, everyone from celebrities to global realtors to sports agents. *B2B Street Fighting*, however, is the first book of its kind to prepare readers to be, in essence, *data geeks* who come prepared with data and background information, both street-level and research-based.

Being a good negotiator is also about trusting your instincts. We'll help you get to know your inner B2B street fighter and learn to trust your intuition – and your data – at the bargaining table, in the corner office, on the sales floor and in the heat of battle.

So forget all you've been taught about negotiation, leave your baggage outside the conference room door and get ready to learn how to approach the bargaining table ready to "float like a butterfly and sting like a bee!"

Punch Lines:

Strategic negotiation is neither a soft skill nor an elective; it is a comprehensive, analytical process that encompasses every department that touches sales.

CHAPTER

3

Problem #1:
Commoditization Pressure

At the negotiating table, the pressure we feel from commoditization is both common and pervasive. It can often be crippling because it limits our options. You think less clearly and have a harder time focusing on your goals. As a result, you make bad decisions – based on temporary conditions – that last, in some cases, forever.

As a refresher, *commoditization* means that everything being sold is essentially the same (at least from the buyer's perspective). You and your competitors are offering the same thing: the same types of technology, the same types of e-learning products, the same types of running shoes, etc. This doesn't mean you don't make the best darn running shoes in the universe, but from a buyer's perspective it's just another running shoe, so why should yours cost more?

The short answer, from your perspective, is that your running shoe is just like a Ferrari. Technically speaking, a Ferrari is just a car. But would a sane person walk into a Ferrari dealership and balk at the sticker price? Hardly. He knows he'll get more than just a car; he'll get state-of-the-art engine technology, cutting-edge comfort, blistering style, out-of-this-world performance and an incredible rush just hearing the engine roar to life. He wouldn't dream of comparing the price of that Ferrari to the price of a Ford Escort, would you? Of course not, because even though the Ferrari is a car, you know it's not a commodity. Yet, in the situation we sellers often face, our buyers approach the negotiation table as if our product *is* a commodity.

> ### Are You Really Selling a Commodity?
>
> To help salespeople determine if they are selling a true commodity, I often ask them:
>
> - Does anyone in your field have a price premium?
> - Does the lowest-priced provider have 100% share?
>
> Ask yourself these questions. If you answer the first question "yes" and the second "no," then you are *not* selling a commodity.

Let's look at another example, this time from both sides. Picture the typical buyer shopping in the marketplace for, let's say, a *widget*. She sees a dozen different boxes – green, yellow, blue, orange, red, etc. – each the same size, weight and dimensions and each containing the same exact thing: an identical widget. All widgets, all the same, differentiated only by box color, which, for the buyer, is an irrelevant detail. How can these widgets be different? They all do the same thing; they widget (whatever that is!)

Of course, the seller of each widget sees things very differently. From his perspective, his unique, one-of-a-kind widget is hardly "just another widget." Company A uses a special alloy developed by its R&D department, so from their perspective, their widget is the Ferrari of widgets; it's completely unique. Company B discovered a way to make its widget twice as strong and half as heavy, two pluses in anyone's book. And both sellers know that these widgets have increased in value with each new alloy, variation on the generic, reduction in size, weight or power consumption, etc., thus truly de-commoditizing them all.

Let's see how each company thinks their widget is different.

- **Company A:** The special alloy developed by this company gives its widget properties that few other widgets can match. The marketing department uses phrases like "one of a kind," "exclusive" and even "brand leader" to bolster Company A's position at the bargaining table. So how can buyers expect to compare the price of this one-of-a-kind, exclusive, brand-leading widget with a plain, old, generic run-of-the-mill widget?
- **Company B:** Twice as strong, half the weight. Two great, key-word-rich taglines and a super countermeasure to use when the negotiation boils down to that inevitable showstopper: price. After all, if Company B's widgets are twice as strong and half the weight as the competition's, why shouldn't they get a price premium?

Clearly, from each seller's perspective, their widgets have value. But to the buyer, the widget itself is not inherently special. What makes it more valuable to this or any buyer, and thus not a commodity, is its impact on their business. For instance, if the special alloy in Company A's widget makes it especially useful in long-running, 50-lollipops-a-second machines or other factory settings where constant use and abuse is a consideration in widget choice, seller A can show a business impact unlike any other for companies with these requirements. Company B's twice-as-strong, half-as-heavy widget makes it the ideal choice for lighter manufacturing companies that are looking to downsize their production lines. For buyers with these needs, Company B's widget is less of a commodity and more of a value-added product.

Expect Buyers to Ante with Commoditization Pressure

Naturally, in any negotiation, it's in the buyer's best interest to at least attempt to commoditize everything you do by saying, "It's all the same, like T-bills or pork bellies…," just like the words "the same thing" in our dread sentence: "I can get *the same thing* cheaper from someone else." When he does this, your product is only differentiated by price (hence the term *price commoditization*).

In our widget example, buyer arguments in favor of commoditization might sound something like these:

- *"I've got three dozen manufacturers all lining up to sell me the same variation of widget. Why should I buy yours if it's 10 cents a unit more than the nearest competitor's?"*
- *"Forget such added value as special alloys, durability, eco-friendliness and the like. A widget is a widget, and I'll take the lowest-priced widget you've got, thank you very much!"*

To these buyers, the fact that the widget might be half as strong or half as durable or twice as likely to stop "widgeting" when they really need it most is *not* more important than low price.

The seller's counterargument might sound like any of these:

- *"After years of research and millions of dollars spent developing the best, strongest and longest-lasting widget on the planet, we are confident our widget will increase your production by 12% and reduce waste by 5%. Isn't that worth 10 cents more per unit?"*

- *"Most of our competitors' widgets are half as strong as ours, so they won't last as long, and they won't perform as well while they do last. Others are twice as heavy as ours, contributing to earlier wear and tear. Our widgets are twice as strong and last twice as long, so at only 10 cents more a unit they are actually cheaper in the long term? Don't you agree?"*
- *"Isn't it worth 10 cents more a unit to boast to your customers that they can market these widgets as eco-friendly: only half as many need to be produced because they last twice as long?"*

In reality, when there is a professional buyer on one side and a professional seller on the other, it's *not* usually a commodity issue, or these professionals would not be involved in the first place. If everything – every widget, every piece of software, every piece of hardware – truly *were* the same and commoditization was a valid argument, you wouldn't need to negotiate at all. You could simply reverse auction your widget, software or hardware on the Internet. There, price prevails and the seller willing to sell at lowest price wins. Sold in this way, a Ferrari would be comparable to a Yugo, and you could score either for two or three grand; but that only makes sense for true commodities.

Whatever the argument – for or against – the fact is that commoditization pressure is just another tactic the buyer uses to back you into a corner so that lowest price becomes the issue rather than quality, customer service, your ability to solve their business problems, a feature they might actually value or a dozen other valuable things you may have to offer. They do this because it works; we feel the pressure and begin to react defensively.

Get ready, B2B street fighters! I'm about to put the power back in your hands. It's time to reframe the conversation to firmly establish that this is not a commodity negotiation.

Value: The Great Commodity Buster

As we saw for Companies A and B, their commodity – a simple widget from the buyer's perspective – became a true standout when selling to companies, for example, the food manufacturers and light manufacturers, who were seeking specific features or could gain from their widget's relevant benefits.

But sometimes a few of your products or services – when compared at the product feature/benefit level – might actually *be* commodities. So what do you do then? Fortunately, when you look at the total business relationship (not just a piece of it) between your firm and the customer, this commodity problem usually goes away.

Let's say, for example, there are two medical device companies, both selling stents. It's easy for the hospital buyer to approach the negotiation saying, "your stent is the same as the competitors." This might be true, but when the negotiation is viewed as the sum of all things that are or could be exchanged as a part of this transaction versus simply as a commodity parts buy, value can usually be created. For example, one supplier may bundle in other products or services, provide better training or support or include some form of data exchange between the hospital and supplier that is critical to using the product or complying with regulations. In other words, the product at the heart of this negotiation *is* a commodity but only until viewed in the context of the supplier's total value proposition.

In another example, let's say you are a medical services distributor and your company offers true commodities like rubber gloves, caps and gowns. In addition to selling these items in bulk from your warehouse, you also offer services such as business process consulting and just-in-time inventory practices. Rather than see the business process consultants and just-in-time inventory services as sideline businesses or as existing in a vacuum, consider them as part of the total picture and you'll soon see they are no longer commodities – to you or your customer.

Viewing supplier companies side-by-side, to see which provides better wrap-around services and support, etc., often reveals a differential that clearly separates the product offerings. Value, then, must be mapped against this customer's needs and viewed from the perspective of the total ecosystem.

Now, if you look at the total relationship between your firm and your customer and it is, in fact, exactly the same as your competitor's relationship, then you don't have a negotiation problem, you have a non-existent value proposition, but we'll save that for another book. For now, we will assume there is some value in what you offer, whether that value is inherent in the product features or design, the ecosystem your company can offer (services, support, delivery times, etc.) or the relationship you bring to the table.

The bottom line? Expect buyers to attempt to commoditize; it's what they're paid to do. And it's the job of the B2B street fighter to combat commoditization at all costs.

To help you do this, it's time to introduce counterpunch #1, consequence of no agreement (CNA) analysis. CNA analysis will give you the skills you need to neutralize commoditization pressure by quantifying what you have that others don't have that is actually valuable to a customer, and leveraging that value to your negotiating advantage. You must be able to articulate value; it's the only thing that will take the pressure off of price and keep the deal from being reduced to a price war over a commodity product or service.

Punch Lines:

Commoditization pressure is just another tactic the buyer uses to back you into a corner so that lowest price becomes the issue rather than quality, customer service, your ability to solve their business problems, a feature they might actually value or a dozen other valuable things you may have to offer.

CHAPTER

4

Counterpunch #1:
Consequence of No Agreement
Analysis

We're ready: on our feet in a fighter's stance with fists up. We expect, in fact, we know the buyer will open the round with some sort of commoditization pressure "punch:" "I can get the same thing … cheaper, faster, better … from someone else." **Counterpunch #1, consequence of no agreement (CNA) analysis**, neutralizes virtually all of a buyer's attempts to commoditize and paves the way for productive and more collaborative discussion about what is really being bought and sold. It guides you through developing your total value proposition and mapping that value to the customer, one deal at a time.

A CNA statement simply describes one alternative a buyer has if the deal with you falls through. It's any reason (or tactic) he presents for not accepting your offer, whether it's true or simply an opening to bargain. Our research on verbal negotiating tactics tells us that in addition to the most common CNA, "I will buy it cheaper from someone else," there are many other common examples of CNA-related tactics you've likely heard over the years.

- "I found someone who can do it faster."
- "We have our own print shop."
- "I'm concerned about late deliveries." (I will choose a supplier with a better delivery record.)
- "Your current/past service is/was poor." (I will choose a supplier with better service.)
- "We have some quality issues or back orders." (I will choose a supplier with higher-quality products.)
- "You know, your competitor's available if necessary."
- "Oh, we do all of that in-house."

While these tactics differ in flavor, they share a common theme: anytime a buyer refers to an alternative to doing business with you such as buying from a competitor, doing a job in-house, or even just doing nothing, he is comparing the value of your offer to the alternatives as he understands them. He is essentially saying that if our deal doesn't close, he can get what he wants elsewhere. The consequences of not reaching agreement with you (hence the name consequences of no agreement) are as good as – in fact better than – your offer, thank you very much!

In the heat of the negotiating battle, these common buyer responses are quite effective tactics, prompting many salespeople to make concessions in order to win the business. Most often, however, the buyer's perspective represented in each CNA is founded on the basis of incomplete facts. From this limited perspective, they view or present their view of your product or service as if it is "the same thing" as everyone else's.

Blueprinting Negotiation, a Start

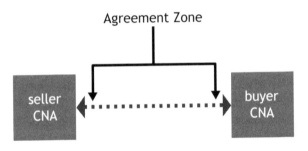

Start blueprinting a deal by mapping out the buyer's and seller's CNAs.

CNA Analysis

In reality, if the two parties don't reach agreement, there will be consequences for both buyer and seller. Notably, you will lose the sale and the buyer loses the opportunity to receive the full value of what your product or business relationship had to offer.

As a modern-day B2B street fighter, your job is to keep this from happening. This where CNA analysis will come in handy. You can use this extraordinarily powerful tool to research and analyze the CNAs for both sides of a specific deal so you can bring a full understanding of your company's unique deal-specific value to the negotiation table. It gives you the ability to provide answers *before* questions are asked.

A world-class negotiator researches, analyzes and understands – in advance – the consequences for both sides of not reaching an agreement, including the soft costs, hard costs and even the possible benefits, both short- and long-term. By determining what will happen should the two sides walk away, the negotiator ultimately gains more power. The side with the better CNA – that is, the one that has less to lose if the deal falls through – naturally has more power.

When CNA analysis is done correctly, tactics based on posturing, bluffing, low-balling and the like suddenly become useless, and buyer decisions or biases based on incomplete data can be revealed for what they are. It enables you to know if a buyer is being truthful when he says he can get the same thing better, faster or cheaper elsewhere, and respond accordingly with facts and knowledge. Without this analysis, your response will just be a reactive shot in the dark. More often, out of necessity, you have been assuming the buyer's tactics are facts, whether they are really true or not.

This is a good time to reiterate that a discussion about CNA analysis is not about price. Of course, price will eventually be part of the negotiation, but first it is imperative that we establish – for ourselves and, to some extent, on behalf of everyone at the table – exactly "what" we are selling before we can have a meaningful discourse about what it's worth.

Keeps the Big Picture in Focus

CNA analysis also helps you keep all the pieces of the deal in context. Most buyers, consciously or not, accept a deal when it's only marginally better than the alternative, and typically without having on hand all the data relevant to the products and value propositions on the table. So when a buyer says, "your stuff is the same as everyone else's," he may actually believe what he is saying, perhaps based on a bad analysis or after comparing only one aspect of your value (for example, only your price, service, flexibility or warranty) to the competitor's. It makes no difference which aspect, as they are all part of the same problem: the buyer is taking one piece of a very complex deal out of context and focusing on it to make their decision.

Your job in this situation, quite simply, is to use the CNA data you collect and analyze to:

- Recognize this tactic for what it is, then
- Bring the overemphasized piece (or aspect) back into context with the overall deal.

CNA Tactic Example

Buyers frequently take one piece of a very complex deal out of context and focus on it to make their decision.

Bring Back into Context

CNA data and analysis help you get all aspects/facts of the deal on the table simultaneously so you can bring the overemphasized aspect back into context with the overall deal and enable more rational business decisions.

Everything we do in this book will help you get ready to do these two things, much to the detriment of non-rational competitors and tough, old-school buyers. To get a preview of what this looks like at street level, let's look at an example.

*A buyer might say, "Hey salesperson, your competitor is so much more flexible than you on delivery dates." How do you bring a decidedly simplistic statement like this back into context? By taking into consideration **all** the other items the buyer needs in order to adequately compare you to the alternative. You might say, "Yes, they may be more flexible on delivery, but they lack a global infrastructure, software to integrate ordering systems and 24/7 support, all of which you've identified as important to your company."*

The key is to anticipate the type of CNA a buyer might use and to push back by having relevant value and competitive data available – and using it!

So what data are we talking about? For starters, information about your own company's value proposition, as well as that of your closest competitor in a specific deal. Understanding and having a working grasp of all the components of the value being negotiated will truly give you a leg up in this process and the ability to put comments, CNA, buyer and competitor reactions in the proper context of the total deal. It's not enough to come back with a retort that's witty but full of hot air; you also have to know, in the example above, that the competitor doesn't provide a global infrastructure and 24/7 tech support in order to emphasize that you do.

The Value of Brainstorming

*Recently a client, the Sales VP of a leading e-learning company, asked me to help with a common problem. "Brian," he said, "we've gotten our butts kicked on the last few deals because everyone says that our competitor is offering **the same stuff at a lower price.**"*

*That's right. This company had heard "I can get the same thing cheaper from someone else" one too many times and was ready to go to the mat so they would never have to hear it again. In short, they were dealing, front and center, with a nasty case of **commoditization pressure**. My team and I agreed to help, and our first step was to make that sentence less scary for them: "Our competitor is offering the same stuff at a lower price."*

Then we kicked off the blueprinting process by getting them to start thinking about their "stuff" in a totally different way.

The first thing I asked this VP was, "When a buyer compares you and your competitor side by side, from the perspective of a purely rational decision maker, what are all the things he should be comparing? Or are your products, in fact, the same?"

The question led to an intense brainstorming session, during which I encouraged this VP and his sales team to start throwing out broad headings that describe their company's stuff, such as learning content or technology. The point was to get the VP and his team to really focus on what his company offers in total relationship to potential customers and competitors.

I can't stress enough the importance of brainstorming like this inside your company – getting to the facts – before attempting to sit down to bargain with the customer. Unfortunately, it's a step most companies skip. Because they treat negotiations emotionally, they focus on preparing themselves mentally (if at all) rather than logically and factually. But I contend that the B2B street fighter who wins most often is not the strongest, the heaviest or even, for that matter, the most qualified. No, he who wins most often is the one who is most prepared.

A Word About Blueprinting

The processes of CNA data collection and analysis that we will learn here as well as trading data and analysis – which we'll cover in the next few chapters – are the first two key steps to what we at Think! call "blueprinting" a deal. Just as you would never dream of starting to build a house without a conventional blueprint, you can't build a deal that is worth negotiating without a plan to get where you are going. Blueprinting is a convenient way to view data-based preparation and analysis in its most basic and raw form; it essentially describes the steps needed to get your arms around all the moving parts in a complex B2B deal. In our experience, blueprinting means more than just planning for negotiation; it *is* negotiation, and helping people blueprint their company or a particular deal is part of how we get them to redefine the processes they use.

CNA Analysis – Let's Get Started

Before beginning to analyze the CNA for any customer or any deal, it's crucial to get a crystal clear understanding of your company's total value proposition. A buyer's CNA statement, by definition, compares your offer to other alternatives, so we need to know exactly how we really compare to others in this deal. To begin, it's often helpful to think of value as the opposite of commoditization; it is the answer to the question "what gives you price premiums?" (since commoditization puts pressure on price).

Then, since value in negotiation is completely relative to the deal on the table, you need to refine your total value to a unique *It*, what you have that this customer wants that the competition does not deliver. A truly unique *It* counteracts all of the buyer's attempts to commoditize since *It* is, by definition, not "the same thing" as what anyone else is offering.

Define a Value Proposition

At this point, I want to stop and state the obvious: I didn't invent the word "value," nor is the concept of selling value a new one. And though no one in modern times would argue with the definition of value – the part of your solution that meets your customer's needs incrementally better than the competition – a big problem remains. For most companies, real, meaningful, bankable value can be a very hard thing to determine.

Just for fun, try polling 10 leaders in your organization by asking them the following questions. What do you think the quality of the answers would be?

- What is the definition of *value proposition*?
- What is *our* value proposition?
- Who owns the care and feeding of our company's value proposition?
- Is there a connection between our value proposition and what our salespeople say and do at the customer level?

Chances are, for every leader you asked, you would get a different, equally qualified response. What do you think the *business impact* of these disparate answers would be, especially given the current state of the economy? If your value proposition is gauzy internally, whether it's unfocused or even unwritten, it will be gauzy to customers as well, putting even more pressure on prices and margins.

We ask these questions a lot. When we ask leaders to define value proposition, they give us very different answers based on their roles. If we ask, "What is *your* value proposition?" we are often handed a laminated card with some esoteric and highly strategic language.

The most common answer to our third question, "Who owns the care and feeding of your company's value proposition?" is usually something like "marketing." When we ask salespeople and sales managers our final question about the connection between their company's value proposition and what salespeople say and do at the customer level, we find that there is virtually *no* connection between what marketing does and how salespeople speak to customers.

In essence, we have found that the core problem many companies have with clarifying value is twofold: first, there is no common company-wide definition of a value proposition and, second, the value statement, when we can find one, is too high level, too static and out of touch with street-level deal making. The result is incoherence about value at the top level and the inability of the salesperson to articulate that value at street level.

I can't put it more simply: when your company is building a business relationship with a customer, your value should represent the sum of all your company's parts that matter … **to this customer**. It should comprise not only the quality of your products and services, but also the commercial language and risk sharing in your contracts, the new products in your pipeline, your overall financial stability, your market image, the human relationships, etc. All these "moving parts" can make defining value difficult, but if you see them *all* as potentially valuable, your perspective becomes much clearer. Unfortunately, this doesn't fit easily on a laminated card.

Conversely, your value for this customer is *not* a long list of all the short- and long-term impacts that you have on multiple levels of a customer's organization. These items – while they represent all the potential components of value you have to offer – belong in a value **pick box** that may or may not be relevant for every deal. The goal is *not* to use all the items in the box for every deal or to throw everything in the box at a customer and see what sticks. Instead, it is to determine what you have that the customer wants or needs, then strategically draw from it the two or three items that achieve this difference in a specific deal. We call this determining your *It* for this deal.

The Four Key Premises of Value

Chances are your company and its products have value, or you'd be out of business by now. And you already know how the inability to clearly articulate meaningful value can impact price pressure and margins when you and your team are selling and negotiating.

Let's get started formulating your value by reviewing some key but often-overlooked premises about value that should help focus and guide you.

1. **Value is incremental.** Too often, executives view value as an esoteric, big picture strategic item when, in fact, customers calculate value based on *their* alternative to you, given *their* needs, not yours. You may have a long list of strategic and tactical items that contribute to your value. It may even be printed on a laminated card! But when it gets to the deal level, only the one or two deal-specific items you have that meet the customer's needs better than the competition make up your true, real-time value.

2. **Value drives price premiums.** Once you know the items that matter to this customer, it's essential to be clear and specific about what you have to offer and present it from the customer's point of view. Only the customer decides how price and risk will be shared based on what your offer is worth to them. In the absence of this well-articulated value he is likely to resort back to some version of "I can get the same thing cheaper elsewhere."

3. **Typically, no single person is responsible for cross-functional and company-wide value.** Without some kind of central focus, a company's value proposition can often be incoherent to those outside, and sometimes inside, the

company. So in many companies, marketing issues a formal statement of company or brand messaging, a list of static bullet points that together detail the value the company can/does offer and to whom.

But the responsibility for delivering most elements of this value are spread out functionally and geographically throughout the company, often in silos with separate profit and loss statements. So, in fact, most components of your company's total value proposition are not centrally owned by marketing or any one department; they are delivered by many people in many departments.

4. **Companies need a living, breathing, evolving value ecosystem.** Value can stagnate. To remain relevant at the street level, it must evolve with your company, with your clients' needs and with the industry. To represent all that your company has to offer, total value must take into consideration all aspects of the company involved in or touched by negotiation, typically sales, finance, legal, operations and marketing. This cross-functional value ecosystem helps to identify total value from multiple perspectives, allows value to grow and flex in sync with the whole company and provides invaluable consultation resources for must-win deals.

Before we get started building your pick box, let's walk through how our e-learning client built theirs.

As we blueprinted with the troubled e-learning VP and his team, we discovered that they had a lot more headings than first imagined. By the end of the first blueprinting session, we had arranged these headings into six broad categories of criteria that a buyer should consider when comparing this firm to its competitor.

Next, we took each broad heading and expanded it with subheadings. Regarding technology, for example, I asked, "What are the hard, measurable elements the buyer should be looking at when comparing your technological advances with those of your competitors?"

The VP's face brightened. "Compatibility!" he shouted. "Our ability to integrate our technology with the client's existing technology," he added, before reeling off qualities such as "reliability, 24-hour tech support and human support."

We were able to quickly fill an entire column under the heading Technology, using specific, measurable items that chipped away at this notion of "same thing." Next, we expanded the other broad headings. Eventually, we came up with 43 items that distinguished this e-learning company from its closest competitor(s).

This list was no fluffed-up resume; every item was fully detailed. There were 43 concrete items that the company saw in a fresh light, perhaps for the first time. This essentially became their "pick box" from which deal-specific value could be derived. By the time we were through, the team saw the full value proposition of their firm and they were able to compare it side-by-side with their competitor's value proposition.

With the pick box full, now they needed to distill their It for a particular deal. Of those 43 items, what things would this particular client not need or value, such as corporate stability or various add-on products like adapters, licenses or updates? What things did the competitors also have, such as 24-hour tech support and live operators on the other end of the line?

The critical goal of the CNA analysis in this example was paring down the large list of 43 items to the two or three that mattered most given the client's needs in this deal, that is, getting a clear picture of what this e-learning company had to sell that this customer wanted or needed, that the competitor didn't.

What was this e-learning company's biggest problem? No surprise, they were facing **commoditization pressure** because clients were comparing apples to oranges. They were getting hammered at the bargaining table because they were seen as just another e-learning company and, after all, don't *all* e-learning companies do the same thing? They all facilitate learning electronically; that is their mission as an industry.

But as you and I both know by now, every e-learning company is different. Some facilitate learning through humor, others with branded, beloved cartoon characters, some with quasi-video games and still others with neat gadgets like pens that do math and memo pads that change colors. Some of these companies are more financially sound than others and have more new products in the pipeline. Yes, they all facilitate learning electronically, but not all means of facilitation or uses of technology or corporate financial health are equal.

Using the basic techniques of CNA analysis, we showed this client how to put its entire potential value on the table, then how to boil down all their stuff – the 43 hard, measurable items – to get to the details of *It* for each deal. I often refer to the process of listing all this stuff as "getting to *It*."

Another phrase for "getting to *It*" that may sound more familiar is finding your true value proposition, and one of our consultants here at Think! Inc. thinks of finding *It* as real-time marketing. For example, when people look at Think! Inc., they see only a training class, and yet we have about 15 products and services that take place before and after the training. So our *It* isn't just training, but all that happens before, during and after the training that no one else does that solves business problems and creates return on investment. You might call it our Ferrari Factor, or what makes us unique, one deal at a time.

As you start the blueprint process for your own company, one thing to keep in mind is that CNA analysis should be done **for every negotiation**, because *It* changes from deal to deal, even though the items on the table are often the same. For example, let's say all the variables, the 43 items in the e-learning company's case, are basically unchanged from one deal to the next. Two or three items are still likely to change, in addition to the fact that this is a differ-ent customer and most likely a slightly different mix of competitors. Translated into action, "getting to *It*" is the simple process of finding the two to three elements in your pick box that constitute the value proposition for this deal. Many times this unique *It* is actually some-thing you built specifically for a deal, something we call Level Three trades, which we'll cover in Chapter 7.

In the next section, I'll walk you through an exercise to complete the pick box of value for your firm, then provide some guidelines for paring it down to the two or three things that form your *It* in a particular deal. You can reuse this pick box data to blueprint many more deals, since the list of things in the pick box does and should evolve over time. What changes in each deal is the *It* that makes your CNA better than the customer's (i.e., their alternative to you). Just like our e-learning example, the goal is to get a clear picture of the *It* that you have that the customer wants and that the competitor doesn't offer.

Example: Defining *It* at Think! Inc.

When my colleagues and I worked through the three-step process to finding *It* for Think!, we used the following broad headings and measurable subheadings.

Pre-Training

- What does the supplier do to diagnose root causes?
- What does the supplier do to engage cross-functionally and set success measurement?
- What kind of tailoring and customization is involved?

Training

- How easy is what we learn in the training to integrate into our other processes (like selling or account management)?
- How much of the workshop is applied to live deals versus generic case studies?
- Are the sales department and all relevant cross-functional players involved in the training?
- How easily is the training assimilated by the team?
- What are the skills of the consultant delivering the workshop?

Post-Training

- When it comes to ability to impact business results, how does Supplier A solve our business problems better than Supplier B?
- What does this company do to assist with coaching and implementing the training?
- Which supplier measures return on investment better?

Blueprinting Your Value

Let's get started filling your pick box. With your company in mind, and using our e-learning example as a guide, let's walk through a three-step process for creating your company's pick box and finding *It* for each deal.

1. **Broad Headings**

   For this first step, you'll need to think like a very rational buyer or groups of buyers, from a variety of different buying influencers inside your customer's organization such as human resources, accounting, etc. Now if you, as the impartial buyer, are comparing your (real) company and it's nearest competitor side by side, what should you be taking into consideration as decision criteria? Think first of the buckets, or broad headings. For instance, with the e-learning firm, these broad headings included technology, content, corporate stability and global reach, but could just as easily have included quality of technical support, reputation, community, relationship, etc.

2. **Subheadings**

   Next, from the perspective of your own company, take a closer look at each heading. Think through the subheadings (that fit under in each heading) that describe how your firm should be compared with another, not from the bias of what your company does well but from the perspective of an analytical decision maker. Choose terms that describe real, tangible things that can be measured at the micro level, not fluffy, vague words that just sound good, like "better quality." For example, subheadings for the heading "technical support" might be "availability, domestic/offshore, cost, etc." It helps to do this using multiple stakeholders within your own organization, for example, what terms would development use, what terms would manufacturing use, etc.

3. **Compare Alternatives to Find *It***

   Now, to find *It*, we compare the alternatives, given the customer's needs for a particular deal. How do you know which items to focus on for a given deal? Essentially, compare and contrast the value points described in the subheadings above to find the few that really make a difference in what you can offer this customer. Throw out things that are not relevant, then compare things on which you are more or less equal. And finally, net out those few things of high importance to the customer where you have an edge.

This analysis needs to be completed objectively. If you can't find anything, dig deeper. If you still can't find *It* – the thing or things that differentiate you on this deal (your real-time value) – then either get ready for a price-only negotiation or change something.

When you do this blueprinting exercise, you're creating the pick box of value for your firm, which you can use for this deal and reuse for many more. This list of things in the box does and should evolve over time, but what changes with each deal is the *It* that makes your CNA better than the customer's CNA (i.e., their alternative to you).

This is a simplistic overview of CNA analysis, a complex, thought-provoking, eye-opening process that companies hire us to facilitate. It is extremely customized to our clients' markets and competitive environments, so providing more detail isn't practical in this book. Suffice it to say that when we complete this process with our customers, we have created a decision guidance tool to help us and them find and refine the two or three things (hopefully more) that they have that their competitors do not have, given the customer's needs in a deal. That is, we have helped them find their *It* for one deal and taught them how to find *It* on their own for deals in the future.

Many years ago, I was a VP of National Sales for Marriott Hotels. When I left to start my consulting firm, the Sales VP at Hilton Hotels hired me for a consulting gig. Now, while I did not reveal any Marriott trade secrets (I still held a lot of stock, after all), I did help the company through one situation. It seems that Hilton's national account teams were told by customers that it had the most inflexible lawyers in the industry.

"That's funny," I said. "Customers used to tell me that Marriott was the worst and Hilton was more flexible!"

Ironically, years before when I was employed by Marriott, I'd heard this same complaint in customer focus groups. In response, I ran back to their Legal Department saying, "You guys have to lighten up; you're killing us with these tough contracts!!!"

The customers' tactic worked; I fell for it! Why? Because I didn't do a good CNA analysis. Any time a customer makes a reference to your competitor or some alternative, it's a CNA tactic.

Value: Keep It Relevant

Mining value to establish the content of a company's pick-box is crucial step to establishing total and baseline value. But value is always relative, so it's important to keep the content updated with new data on your products and company, your competitors' products and company and the market in which you do business. On a deal-by-deal basis, you can then select the items relevant to each deal.

Finding your *It* is what gives you the edge, the power and the price premiums. This type of netting out analysis should be completed for each deal, using your pick box of value, because the people, the context and the issues surrounding every negotiation are different. There are no market-level analyses, only deal-level analyses. In fact, your *It* is the only reason price premiums exist, unless a buyer does something stupid and overpays – and I can't figure out how to write a book on making buyers consistently do that! However, I *can* write one that helps you consistently get price premiums or, at the very least, avoid wasting time on those deals where you can't.

Never Negotiate Scared Again

Now when a buyer provokes a reaction by taking a single piece of the negotiation and focusing on it out of context, you'll be ready. Perhaps your competitor is a little faster than you, in which case a buyer's CNA might sound like, "I can get faster products from someone else." The data collected and analyzed told you that that speed is not the customer's number one priority and that you are better on three other attributes that they value more. This empowers you to easily neutralize speed as an issue of concern (commoditization pressure), and prepares you put this item back into context with the total negotiation. Remember that much of negotiation has to do with staying calm under pressure and acting rather than reacting. Preparation allows you to view all the pieces of the deal, in motion, in real time, without making mountains out of molehills.

The knowledge gained through CNA analysis also helps with the balance of power in a negotiation. Most sellers assume that the buyer has more power in every deal simply because it's the buyer who is paying the seller in some fashion for goods or services. But a thorough CNA analysis will show when this is not actually the case. For example, if your sales organization is the incumbent, the cost to the buyer of switching to another supplier might be prohibitive. Here you actually do have more power. I could give numerous examples of how the buyer doesn't always have the power in the negotiation, but the point is that without a CNA analysis you probably won't know.

Would it surprise you to know that many times the seller and the customer have unclear or incomplete ideas about what's being bought and sold. Is *It* training or support after training? Is *It* funky gadgets or cutting-edge technology? Arguing over *It* is difficult when the sides have different concepts of what *It* means. CNA analysis ensures that at the very least *you* will be very clear what *It* is and its value to the buyer.

Perhaps you've noticed that at no time during this discussion of CNA analysis have I mentioned price. That's because this first step is all about defining *It* **before** we discuss price or, in other words, what the customer will pay for *It*. Once we are all in agreement about what's being sold, we can begin to talk about the price of that offering. That's coming up in the next few chapters, when we discuss counterpunch #2. Once price does become an issue, you will be well prepared, thanks to your CNA analysis, to counterpunch with the unique solution mix that nobody else has in this deal.

Imagine a revitalized conversation between that e-learning company Sales VP and his next negotiating nemesis. It might go a little something like this:

"But have you seen Cyber Student's talking, blinking magic pen?" asks the buyer.

"Yes, I have," explains our fearless Sales VP. *"I've also seen its sticker price; buying one new unit from Cyber Student is equivalent to buying three of our top-selling programs, and the magic pen is only compatible with their premium package, an upgrade to what you are considering. Our proposed Lunar Learning module gives your customers similar technology with* **no** *upgrades, because it is compatible with all of our existing e-learning products."*

See how part of the e-learning VP's confidence level comes from knowing his competitor's products so well – in addition to knowing his own **It***?*

Most salespeople can readily do their own CNA analysis, but not the analysis for the other side. The consequence of not doing this is selling or negotiating scared! The unprepared salesperson will assume the buyer always has the power and will likely overstate the impact of losing the deal. It might sound a little like this: "If I lose this deal, I miss quota. If I miss quota, I don't get my bonus. If I don't get my bonus, my daughter doesn't get braces and will have crooked teeth. Crap! I better get this deal at all costs!" Not exactly a calm, prepared, professional stance from which to negotiate.

It's kind of like walking into a dark alley, seeing three thugs and getting that sinking feeling. Now, imagine walking into that alley with 10 years of martial arts training, 20 extra pounds of muscle, a baseball bat in one hand and nun-chucks in the other. Seeing those three thugs now it's likely you will have a very different, more confident response.

Having CNA data on hand during negotiations prepares you to keep the power and to keep the buyer focused on what matters. In almost every business deal where we have done CNA analysis for both sides of the table, there is more shared power than absolute power, in fact, we have more power than we thought. This gives us more confidence and prepares us to take control of the negotiation and educate the other side.

We also find that when most buyers state that the alternative is better, faster or cheaper, it's simply not true. It's not that they are lying, per se, but they typically have not thought through their CNA

■ CNA Analysis Helps Keep Everyone's Eyes Open

I was working with the procurement department at a major insurance company that was sourcing asset management software. At the start of the meeting they said, "We want a 7% price reduction on our current $12 million spend; that's our goal and strategy."

I said okay and started with a CNA analysis, the insurance company's first. "What are the consequences to you if this deal falls through?" I asked.

"Well, we would have to go to another vendor," they answered.

So I asked, "Who is the most likely alternative?"

Their response was "Asset Soft, Inc. We have their proposal, it came in at $18 million. Quite frankly, the costs of switching are high, and we think the software requires more people to manage than another software solution."

"How can it be," I asked, "that your current vendor is already priced lower than someone you think is not as good?"

Their response was that several years ago they were the incumbent software company's first customer and, but for them, the software firm wouldn't exist.

I asked about now, "Don't you think the world has changed over the years? Don't you think the CNA of your supplier is to replace you with another customer willing to pay at least $18 million, if they are indeed better than the next-best vendor? And yet you want them to accept a deal at $11 million?"

They saw the point and, hopefully, so do you. This was a group of professional procurement officers in a Fortune 100 company who were irrationally going after this massive price reduction with little or no analysis beyond the fact that they were told to reduce the company spend by 7%. Sadly enough, this tactic may have actually worked with the supplier, especially if the supplier didn't do a complete CNA analysis on the insurance company to know that their acquisition price and operating costs were going to be higher to move to a different supplier's solution.

clearly. When we do the analysis properly, we are actually *helping* them make better decisions.

The "same thing" Is Not What You Sell!

Let's look back and see how CNA analysis helps you diffuse our famous sentence: "I can get the same thing cheaper from someone else." Through meticulous collection of data and careful analysis we've begun solving the elusive "same thing" dilemma by:

1. Clarifying the *Its*: What does the client want to buy, what are you selling, what is the competitor offering. More importantly, CNA analysis nets out the services/products that you have that the buyer wants that the competition cannot offer.
2. Keeping the negotiation focused on the facts: Facts, not emotions or verbal tactics, are at the heart of a CNA analysis. It helps us figure out and stay focused on the real facts.

"Just the Facts, Ma'am"

It's not enough to **gather the facts and know the facts**, what's most important is that you also **face the facts**. Doing a thorough, fact-finding CNA analysis is the only way to come to the bargaining table fully prepared. Otherwise, it's like bringing a switchblade to an AK-47 shootout!

Rational, fact-based diagnoses for rational, fact-based decision making benefits everyone. Facts not only help you formulate the winning *It* for this deal, they gives you a heads up when the unexpected happens. For example, there are times when the *It* on the table is much more valuable, in terms of working parts, than the client perceives. Other times, you realize the client's alternative is better and perhaps you need to rethink your value or walk away. That's okay, because I'd rather have you walk away from a deal after doing an analysis than have you do a bad deal because you never got around to the analysis in the first place.

Don't be afraid to learn that your competitor *also* offers 24-hour support, excellent customer service, complete compatibility or state-of-the-art technological advances. After all, they have those things whether you know about them or not. *Not* knowing might make you feel like king of the mountain, but you're in for a big shock at the bargaining table when some professional buyer calls you out on your claims and points to these facts about your competitors … not quite the power play you were hoping for.

And remember, the buyer sees your offer as a gain or loss depending on how they view their alternative to you, their CNA. So when they don't know the full scope of this alternative and start focusing on one piece of the deal out of context, your job is to have and use all the data to educate them before you make any offers. You could throw value-creating offers on the table all day long, but if the buyer has incorrectly diagnosed their alternative, you're just not going to get this deal done. Take a step back, help the buyer understand the total consequences of not reaching agreement with you and *then* put your offer on the table. (More on that in the next two counterpunches.)

CNA Quick Reference

The critical goal of the CNA analysis is getting a clear picture of the *It* that you are selling and that the customer is buying, as well as what the competitor is offering. Then on a deal-by-deal basis, find the two or three items your company has that the competitor doesn't, given the client's needs in a deal. Before we move on to establishing a price for your *It*, here is a quick summary of the steps for completing a CNA analysis:

- Choose the most likely alternative for the customer of not reaching agreement with you. This is usually either your competitor, doing nothing or choosing a substitute. If the customer has two to three choices, start with the most likely one.
- Completely analyze everything the customer should be taking into consideration when he compares you to those alternatives, creating a list similar to the 43 items the e-learning company brainstormed during its blueprinting session. It is key to adopt the mindsets of multiple players in your customer organization: buyer, technical, finance, operations, legal, etc.

(basically, employees in any cross-functional department who are impacted by this deal).

- Compare the alternative to your total value proposition and find the one or two (or hopefully four or five) items that will compel the customer to choose you.

- Do a quick analysis of the impact to your company if you lose this deal. I'll admit, most times it's a pretty depressing exercise, but often you'll find some positive impacts like losing a low margin customer, sending a message to the market that you're playing tougher or jettisoning a high maintenance customer.

At every step, don't be shy about sharing data with your customers; present the data as a way of helping them make better, more informed decisions. At Think! we do this often, usually by saying something like: "We know our competitor is Lakeside Group. This is what we like about them and how they fit your needs on this deal; however, here are two or three key areas where they fall short and where we can help."

CNA analysis is an integral part of negotiation, not just a way of planning for it. When you're doing this work, you are in essence pre-negotiating, in some ways defining if not designing where you think this negotiation should begin.

Punch Lines:

A thorough CNA analysis neutralizes virtually all of a buyer's attempts to commoditize and paves the way for a productive and more collaborative discussion about what is really being bought and sold. It gives you the ability to provide answers before questions are asked.

CHAPTER

5

Problem #2: Price Pressure

We've talked about how to use CNA analysis when a buyer attempts to commoditize your offering. Now we get to the big whale: price pressure. It is probably fair to say that price pressure is the sucker punch, the knockout punch or the pick-your-own-favorite-pun-if-you're-tired-of-mine of B2B negotiation.

Price pressure is the second most common negotiation problem facing modern businesses today. In fact, it is so pervasive that it has become a kind of self-fulfilling prophecy. The more you hear the word *price* from people who want you to focus on it (to the exclusion of just about everything else going on at the bargaining table), the more you consciously and unconsciously start to think about one thing and one thing only: price.

I think we can agree that the chance of you hearing the following statement is approximately zero: "Well, (insert your name here), I've been looking at your proposal, and your prices are just too low relative to the competition's. Can you raise them?"

Or maybe: "I've been looking at the contract, and your terms have you taking on way too much risk. Can we shift some of that risk back to me?"

Or even: "I really want to talk about the services you provide. You're not charging me for those, and I think you should."

Not only are you unlikely to hear any of those comments from your clients, you're almost certainly going to hear the exact opposite:

- "Lower your price."
- "Your contract is just too difficult."
- "Everyone else includes that service free."

So why then are we knocked back on our heels each and every time this happens? I believe one reason is that we have blindly accepted the notion that we can never know what's going to happen in negotiation, so we don't even think about how to prevent these scenarios from happening in the first place. Another reason is that we simply haven't collected enough data, and that's because we don't know:

- what data to collect
- how to use it when we have it

By far the most common form of concession pressure, price pressure occurs anytime you're asked to give *something* away for free. Typically it begins when a buyer focuses on one aspect of a deal, then ends up parsing that one thing into smaller components and asking for concessions for each component. It might be a price reduction or a request to give away something for free – a service, a specific contract term, legal terms or a condition in which the buyer is asking you to take on all the risk in a deal. For the seller, this is a zero sum game. The buyer has not only lost track of the big picture of the deal, but in doing so stopped considering the potential value of other components of the deal.

Let's look back at some statistics from our SAMA research with global account managers that demonstrate just how pervasive this practice is.

- **92% say they are seeing more professional buyers.** We're seeing more professional buyers out there, largely because of the economy and because companies want to lower costs as a way of increasing profits. We can count on the fact that a buyer's core competency is negotiating; ours is selling. We are immediately up against someone who is prepared to make harsh demands on price and other value-deflating giveaways, and if we're unprepared we'll be outmanned and outgunned.
- **91% say buyers are increasingly focused on price and give-aways.** 84% are feeling more pressure to give things away for free or better!
- **81% say their competitors are acting irrationally.** Buyers are slamming the competition for free stuff, and the competition is complying, putting huge pressure on all sellers going after a deal to give away more.

These statistics clearly support the notion that price negotiation is much tougher right now, and given the current economic downturn, it's not likely to get easier anytime soon. But before we introduce counterpunch #2 to solve this problem, let's be sure we're clear about the many ways that your clients can ask for free stuff (as opposed to just saying, "Give us free stuff!").

There Are Many Words for "Free"

For many years we have been asking our global clients for the most common and most difficult verbal negotiation tactics they face every day. Their buyer's comments may sound different, but they all have one thing in common. Whether buyers are asking for a price discount, an extended warranty or some other concession, the message is loud and clear: they want something, they want it now and they want it for free or less! From our research and from what we have observed, they are very likely to get it!

Here is just a small sample from our surveys of the thousands of tactics buyers have used to ask for some concession from sellers.

- The tendency to compartmentalize negotiations around one aspect (like price) and not look at the big picture of contract benefits
- The refusal to recognize our value add, even though they use it, and the focus on price
- Asking and assuming this is just the start: What's the discount? What's the real price?
- The price is too high
- I have no money right now
- Your share requirements are too high
- Your amenity values are inflated
- No budget
- Our goal is to cut our costs by 10% over the previous contract
- We have some major problems with meeting service level agreements, etc.
- Budget limitations

- Our business model does not allow us to pay that type of premium
- This decision will be made based solely on price
- We cannot close these deals at these price points
- Lead times are long; let's get these prices locked in so we can stock your items and avoid lead times
- This is what we want
- Your price is too high
- The most important thing is price
- We are looking for the best price
- How much can you bring the price down?
- Is that the final price?
- Need to do better with the price
- If you can't reduce the price, you will be kicked out of the bid
- If you do not lower the price, then we are going elsewhere with our business
- The customer wants a price up front, even before we have had the opportunity to create value
- Rebates
- 10% off last price paid
- Lowest price wins

Was that painful enough? Do any of these sound like comments you've heard lately? In fact, about half of all global tactics were similar in that the buyer attempted to force a concession by picking one aspect and focusing on it out of context. If this sounds familiar, that's because it is the same problem that cropped up earlier in our discussions about commoditization pressure and CNA analysis. If I pound one thing into your street-fighter head, let it be this: business deals should be evaluated by both sides based on all the data for both sides. We can't take one piece out of context; it just doesn't make sense.

The good news is that there is an easy way to counter all these buyer tactics once you recognize them for what they are. Counter-punch #2, trading, is asking for something in return when a buyer makes a demand of you. It is the key, now more than ever, to bringing the price of what you are offering back into context.

If we, as negotiators, made this simple but highly effective change to our negotiation strategy, profit margins in our companies would skyrocket while actually providing some benefit to our customers. Just as we have to change the way we're negotiating, buyers also have to recognize that, for most of us, margins are down. Demanding that we give away more margin simply does not fly anymore.

In the next chapter we'll use trading to move the conversation away from price and toward other, more valuable features. You'll see how trading can be used even with professional buyers who are consistently (or cagily) resistant to logic. It will arm you with enough data to fight back against a small army of angry purchasing agents!

There is an easy way to counter buyer tactics once you recognize them for what they are. Trading is the act of asking for something in return when a buyer makes a demand of you. It is the key to bringing the price of what you are offering back into context.

Punch Lines:

There is an easy way to counter buyer tactics once you recognize them for what they are. Trading is the act of asking for something in return when a buyer makes a demand of you. It is the key to bringing the price of what you are offering back into context.

CHAPTER

6

Counterpunch #2:
Trading

Most buyers attempt to minimize the complexity of negotiation by simply saying, "Well, the other side's price is lower." This is like trying to make a decision with the majority of the criteria missing. We all know that price is a function of many things: how much volume is being purchased, what products and services are included, who is assuming more risk and so on. So our job as professional negotiators is to get past a buyer's fixation on price and put all the moving parts on the table simultaneously, empowering both sides to make well-informed business decisions.

Once you've completed a CNA analysis and agreed on what's being sold, it's time to determine what the ideal terms look like for both sides. **Counterpunch #2, trading**, helps you keep all the pieces of a deal in context, so you can keep the conversation away from price alone. Put simply, trading is the art of asking the buyer for something in return when he makes demands of you – whether for a lower price or other concessions.

Trading is the heart and soul of negotiating. Done well, it combats pressure from the buyer to reduce the price of a deal or give away all manner of "stuff" for free, and sometimes less. If you think of CNA analysis as defining *It*, then trading analysis is getting clarity on what total economic costs, risks and benefits the buyer will pay and seller will accept for *It*.

Most buyers are also looking for solutions to problems or enhance-ments to their value chain. Trading also enables you to assist these buyers in solving problems or improving processes, creating value for both sides.

It's important that you not let this next stage, a discussion of terms, become an oversimplified discussion of price. Even when price is a buyer's singular focus, there is just too much value at stake for both sides to ignore the other interdependent, moving parts of this deal. Remember, money is just one aspect of negotiation, not the be-all and end-all. There are many currencies in a B2B deal.

Trading analysis is basically just what it says: an analysis of what each side wants from a deal, what each side wants to keep out of the deal, what each side is willing to trade to close the deal and the priority of all the items in question. One of the important tasks accomplished through trading is managing the economic and risk elements associated with *It*. This could include pricing on all relevant products, services, volume, length of contract, type of service and support, warranty, terms and conditions and more. Unfortunately,

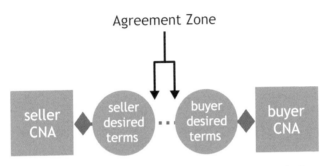

Trading helps you establish the desired terms of the deal for both buyer and seller.

much like CNA, many times buyers don't come to the table prepared to talk about anything but price. In fact, in most negotiations with which my firm assists, both sides come to the table without having done their homework on these two key data points:

1. *What are the alternatives to reaching agreement (CNA) look like for both sides?*
2. *What are the total terms/trades of the deal to be agreed upon?*

Creating Value for Both Sides

So what business problem does trading solve? Well, let's break out our scary negotiating sentence: "I can get the same thing (commoditization pressure) cheaper (price focus) from someone else." As you can see, trading helps you fight back against the business problem of **price focus** when the other side of the table throws the c-word (cheaper) around.

Your closest competitor may, in fact, seem cheaper at first, so you have to dig deep to see what you're willing to trade in order to level the playing field, then tip the scale in your favor. It all goes back to challenging that firefighter or moving target mentality so many of us have as we stride up to the bargaining table. We fixate on price to the exclusion of all other aspects of a deal.

In a way, fixating on price is like preparing for a street fight by only doing bicep curls on one arm. You ignore the other arm completely, not to mention the legs, the abs, the glutes, the cross-training, the cardio, all of it – just so you can have one big arm for one big punch. But the minute your competitor sees that big Popeye arm, all of your single-minded training will be for naught because your intentions will be so obvious. He will quickly learn to avoid that one massive arm and spend the rest of the fight repeatedly striking blows to your many vulnerable spots.

Thorough trade data collection and analysis leaves you with very few weak spots because you're always creating leverage in the deal by finding ways to trade things *other* than price. In fact, *many* items can be traded to optimize the deal for price and provide value across the board; the key is to think them through in advance. Remember: fire prevention first aids firefighting later.

In the last chapter, findings from our research clearly showed mounting price pressure from every type of buyer:

- **92% say they are seeing more professional buyers.**
- **91% say buyers are increasingly focused on price and giveaways.**
- **81% say their competitors are acting irrationally.**

That same research also showed that **79% of respondents say that they are not good at trading**, so there are a lot of sellers out there missing out on the opportunity to punch back hard enough to hurt their competitors – not to mention adding value for their clients. Let's examine why trading is so critical to deal making.

If a client asks you for a $500 price decrease and you agree, all you have done is take $500 from your wallet and put it into his. The world-class street fighter is averse to shifting value but very adept at trading items that cost less than the value they provide to the client, that is, at creating value.

The first step in creating value through trading is this pre-work to understand what the ideal trading items are. It is the pre-work, in fact, that actually enhances the value that is being negotiated in a deal versus simply shifting value from one party to another. Creating value for trading is actually good for both sides.

Before we learn how to trade, I want to remind you that the buying company, typically simplified in this book to "buyer," actually represents multiple buying influences within the customer's company. I don't want you to lose sight of the fact that, just as you represent multiple parties on the seller's side of deal, the buyer across the table *always* represents multiple people, departments and buying influences with a stake in this transaction. This fact becomes very important during trading analysis and will play an important role in the next counterpunch as well.

Earlier, I mentioned the IACCM, the International Association of Contract and Commercial Managers, an association of professional contract negotiators on the buy and sell side with whom we work closely. In their experience, there is typically a salesperson who sells to and manages an account. She comes to agreement with a customer, deems the deal sold, then turns the deal over to the contract manager. At this point, usually the **It** *the customer is buying and how much he is paying for* **It** *have already been agreed upon, and now it's the contract manager's job to negotiate all the terms and conditions.*

Frankly, this is a ridiculous idea. I'm not referring to the contract manager, of course, but to the surgical turnover while all the potential tradable items in a deal are being negotiated. It puts both the buyer and the seller in a very precarious situation. On the front end, the salesperson feels price pressure but lacks the risk items on the back end to trade for price. It also challenges the contract manager on the back end, who doesn't have price to trade because that's already been agreed upon. At the end of the day, it's all just a bunch of zero-sum risk shifting.

This is how most people think about negotiation, and unfortunately, it's the way most big companies are set up. Negotiation is turned over to contract managers with little cross-strategizing with salespeople. In the end, the deal is done but tons of trading opportunities were left on the table, putting more pressure on price.

My poor friends, the contract managers, are getting killed as a result of this strategy. Or should I say, non-strategy. Robustness (or complexity or whatever we want to call it) is at the core of B2B negotiation. To create maximum value for both sides, we want as many moving parts as possible for leverage and for setting up a variety of creative trades (take a little here, give a little there). Recall the theme here: the natural complexity of B2B deals is your friend as well as the enemy of commoditization. We need to embrace it and organize around it more efficiently than everyone else, not make strategic decisions that reduce or ignore it.

A Trading Primer

Our deal is going through; so now we're ready to talk "terms," that is, we're ready for trading analysis. Trading gives us a powerful way to determine what both buyer and seller really want so we can use these things in the next counterpunch to make each deal more productive and profitable.

In a nutshell, each side creates a prioritized list of the top three or four items they need, want or value from the other side, items that one side values more or less than the other side can be traded, and measurable business value is created. Just to get you warmed up, here is a simple example of trading in action.

First, prepare because you know it's coming: the client says, "You need to lower your price by 10%."

Then you say, "Sure, there might be a path to that. How about we increase volume or length of contract?"

Most deals have a few levels of trades that include the following:

- **Level 1 Trades:** *Basic prices for products and services included in the deal.* These are the usual suspects at the heart of most deals, such as:
  - price
  - volume
  - services
  - products
  - warehousing
- **Level 2 Trades:** *Terms and conditions of the deal.* These include such high-level items as:
  - legal terms
  - conditions
  - raw materials clauses
  - length of contract
  - cancellation fees
- **Level 3 Trades:** *Creative trades.* These are outside-the-box elements that one side values greatly and that don't cost the other side too much. Level 3 trades can really change a business relationship, turning a deal from buy/sell to alliance/partnership. They are the mark of world-class negotiators.

Most seasoned negotiators we work with do not complete thorough blueprinting of Level 1 and Level 2 trades for both sides. But to achieve Level 3 trades, you first need to effectively manage Level 1 and Level 2 trades, getting them all on the table at once. Better organization of Levels 1 and 2 will definitely help you fight fires, but Level 3 trades help you prevent them!

With these three levels of trades in mind, here's a quick overview of how to complete a trade analysis.

- **Seller side:** Think through the different trades valued by multiple players on the seller's (your) side of the deal. What kind of products do the product managers want? What services does the service team want? What kind of clauses does legal want? What pricing does the sales manager or finance want?

  Do this analysis for all three levels of trades: products and services, terms and conditions and creative/custom trades for this deal that move your relationship from seller to alliance partner.

- **Buyer side:** Think through all three levels of trades for multiple buyers on the customer's side of the deal (e.g., the professional buyer, executives, lawyers, technology people) asking questions similar to those on the seller side.

- **Rank the trades:** Once you have compiled these lists for multiple influencers on both sides of the deal, take a stab at determining what is most-to-least important, how important the top items are and what priority ranking (high to low) each side is likely to ask for and accept.

Trade Tactic Example

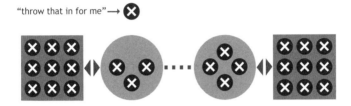

Even during trading it is easy for clients to take one aspect of the overall deal or one trade out of context.

Bring Back into Context

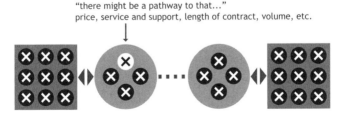

Trading analysis helps get and keep all aspects of the deal on the table simultaneously because each aspect, e.g., price, is now a function of many other variables

The Holy Grail: Level 3 Trades

Several times I've mentioned that robustness and complexity are at the heart of B2B negotiations. I hope by now you are beginning to see that the many moving parts of each deal give us the leverage we need to set up a variety of creative trades. It is this same robustness that makes Level 3 trades such a powerful way to close win-win deals and create value for both sides.

To get you thinking about Level 3 trades, here's an example:

Two sides were doing a great job of uncovering all the variables in Level 1 and Level 2 negotiables. Next, they brainstormed possible creative Level 3 negotiables, items not currently on the table and presumably not part of the negotiation. Brainstorming led to suggestions for using the relationship to grow the top lines of both firms, which opened up a discussion of consumer databases and marketing. The two sides realized that one had a segment of the market in their database that the other valued. They agreed to marry the databases and develop a joint consumer marketing program.

This Level 3 creative trade diverted more costs to the buyer (for developing a new database) than lowering prices of the actual product. It generated more revenue for the seller (with the marketing program) than any margin improvement or charging higher prices would have achieved.

Level 3 trades make it much more difficult for buyers to focus solely on price. This is so important that I want to say it again: *Level 3 trades make it much more difficult for buyers to focus solely on price.* The word "cheaper" usually refers to the acquisition price or the price per unit when negotiating pure commodities, where the focus is solely on price or price aligned with volume. In a Level 3 trade, we are negotiating solutions, so it is almost impossible and certainly illogical to take one piece of the overall negotiation out of context because price is now a function of many other variables. Most of us know the difference between the acquisition price per unit and the TCO. Price is what we've *been* negotiating; Level 3 Trade changes the dialogue to a negotiation based on TCO, which is what we *should be* negotiating.

Trading data also affects the balance of power in the same way that CNA data did during CNA analysis in Chapter 4. Once you make a Level 3 trade in a deal, it changes the CNA for you as well as for the customer. Specifically, it makes the many moving parts of the deal more interdependent, making it harder to replace either party if an agreement is not reached. Getting to Level 3 also promotes face time with the professional buyer's internal customers, an extremely important benefit we will touch on in the next chapter.

Most buyers are also looking for solutions to problems or enhancements to their value chain, and Level 3 Trades enable sellers to assist buyers in solving problems or improving processes. Take steel, for example. A buyer could easily say that concrete is cheaper than steel, but when one looks at the CNA, at the cost of maintaining the two over time and at the expected life of each, it is easy to see that steel is superior over a longer time period. Other economic and risk elements such as volume, length of contract, type of service and support and warranty also determine price. A seller who refuses to focus on price alone is not playing hardball; he's being logical.

In summary, remember that Level 3 trades involve items **that are not currently on the table and presumably not part of the negoti-ation**. It is this type of higher-level trade that signals a more strategic negotiation. Remember, too, that you won't find Level 3 trades **for all deals**. In fact, managing Level 1 and Level 2 trades effectively is what you need to do first – and what isn't done on most deals.

This Salesman's Best Friend

Often, even something that looks like a commodity situation can be broadened into an opportunity to create value. By treating my recent rental experience as if it had the moving parts of a B2B deal – it was easy to create a better deal and value for both sides.

I own an rental apartment in Chicago in the building where I live. When an old tenant leaves, I run an ad to fill the vacancy. Very often the negotiation for the rental comes down to price. To counteract that and, because I'm a dog lover (and owner), I *always offer the same discount in the ad: the rent is $1,400 per month without a dog and $1,350 with a dog.*

Now, I know what you're thinking: $1,350 is pretty cheap for a Chicago apartment. But here's my way of thinking: As a dog lover, I want to give other dog lovers a break since most landlords will not rent to them. More selfishly, however, I'm often on the road, and I know that a dog lover is probably more willing to be a dog sitter as well. So my reasons were really twofold from the start.

Most people call to confirm that the ad is a mistake: the price is low without a pet, even lower with a dog? But my answer is always the same: "$1,400 per month without a dog and $1,350 with a dog."

The first time I ran this ad, a woman named Maxine called and said she'd take the apartment. It turned out Maxine ran a mobile dog grooming service for busy city dwellers. She told me, "Brian, anyone who's this dog friendly, well, I want to live in your building." But she had a question first: "I've got two dogs, does that mean I get the apartment for $1,300?"

I had to admit, I got a chuckle out of that! Then I thought for a minute and asked, "Well, Maxine, that depends. What do you charge to groom dogs?"

*The negotiator in me was already thinking: I can make a valuable **trade** with Maxine so we both get something we want out of this deal. She gets the rent she wants, but instead of just conceding out of habit or giving something away without getting something in return, I get a valuable service out of the deal. You see, I already get my dog groomed every so often anyway. That means traipsing all over town, waiting around, getting back home with the dog still clean, etc. It's a real hassle! Suddenly a dog groomer was thinking about moving into my building, and not just the same building, but my rental apartment. This could work out beautifully for us both. Then it also occurred to me that I might not have to send my spoiled rotten dog to playgroup anymore if he could play with Maxine's dogs instead. And in our discussions we realized that we both employed dog walkers, so we could probably start covering for each other!!!*

So here's the math on this one. First, we list tradable items and establish the value of each item to both sides.

- Shampoo costs = $25 for her and $50 for me (rent)
- Shampoo value = $85 to landlord
- Playgroup cost = $50 reduction in Maxine's rent
- Playgroup value = $300 to landlord
- Dog walker cost = $50 reduction in Maxine's rent
- Dog walker value = $100 ($50 each)

Then we divide joint value, given concerns for fairness in the ongoing relationship.

- Maxine's rent was lowered by $200, and in the end she paid a monthly rent of $1,200. She also acquired a new customer worth $25 over her costs. **A net value to her of $225/month.**
- I conceded $200 in rent but saved: $85 in dog grooming, $300 in playgroup costs, and $50 in walking services. **A net value to me of $235/month** (over the $1,200 rented apartment).

This is a great example of trading, because it is a net gain for both sides. In effect, we get built-in dog sitting, avoid the cost of a professional dog walker when either of us is away, plus my dog now gets playmates. More formally (for those keeping score), the official trades were:

- Maxine wanted to move in; I offered the rental at **$1,350** with a dog.
- Maxine said, "Hey I'm a groomer." I was paying $85 to have my dog groomed and she charged $100. At face value, we both would have walked away from this until I looked at the hassle of dropping off and picking up my dog and she looked at her cost, $25. We agreed to have her groom my dog for $50, and my cost would be lowering her rent by $50 to **$1,300.**

- *Another inherent trade developed as we started talking: I paid for doggy playgroup because I figured my dog could play with her dogs all day long. This cost her nothing, while I valued the service at $300. So I lowered the rent another $50 to **$1,250**.*
- *We could mostly cover each other for dog walking services when I was traveling or when she was working late, which costs us both nothing. We figured the total value to me was about $100, so I lowered the rent another $50 to **$1,200**.*

When you're blueprinting a trade, you have to ask yourself: *What are the total terms of the deal beyond price – for multiple people on both sides of the table?* They should include price, quality, services, the total terms of the entire deal and all three levels of trades.

In contrast, I'll juxtapose how this negotiation would have looked as a one-item rent or priced-based negotiation. If I ran a typical ad for $1,400 and people didn't want to pay that much rent, they could ask me for a lower price. If I agreed to $1,350, all I did was take $50 from my wallet and put it into theirs.

By broadening the terms of the deal, Maxine and I found services that cost less than the value they provided and literally grew the size of the deal, eventually providing me $435 worth of trades at a cost of $200, creating $235 of extra value by trading! This is the best way to counterpunch price or any other giveaway pressure.

If I had compared Maxine with my old dog groomer on price alone, the price-focused math would work out with Maxine at $100 and my old groomer at $85. So without a CNA analysis (all the hassles of transporting the dogs back and forth, free dog walking, etc.), I would have said she is more expensive than the competition. But *after* CNA analysis – determining the *It* she really offered – I quickly found out that I **can't** get the same thing cheaper elsewhere. (By the way, I think it's important to note here that her service is mobile dog grooming. She picked up and dropped off my dog instead of me having to do all the leg work.)

By the same token, if Maxine had looked only at my offer of $50 for grooming, she would have said, "Forget it. I can get $100 elsewhere." But when she factored in all the other trades we were making on rent, convenience, the dog-friendly apartment, as well as CNA analyses for both sides, the total terms of this deal made it more attractive than merely comparing offers on price alone. A salient point here is that if I can do this in an apparent B2C commodity situation and fairly simple sale, the possibilities for using trading and CNA data in B2B deals are virtually limitless.

Important Considerations for Trading

It's key to remember that there are multiple people on your side of the deal and multiple influencers on the customer's side of the deal, all of whom have trading items of interest. Rarely do they have *all* the trade data handy in one place. By thinking through many of the deal items in advance, you can literally take proactive control of the negotiation. Even if you're only 50% to 60% accurate, you still will likely have more data than your customers or competitors.

As we saw in my apartment example, trading can also create more value than either side anticipated going into the negotiation, in effect expanding the pie before it's divided. The well-seasoned negotiator understands that his goal in fact should be to create joint value; trading allows this to happen. For example, if the buyer places great value on direct store delivery and the seller already has a route that covers the area, the seller can provide the service at very little cost. He can easily trade this item for something that the other side controls, such as a higher price or less stringent service requirements.

When one of our technology clients began trading (as opposed to giving away stuff for free) with one of the most difficult hardware manufacturers in the business, it was a shift from 20 years of doing hundreds of millions of dollars of deals together. When this deal was over, the customer asked our client, "What was different this time?"

In reply, our client asked, "What do you mean?"

The customer replied, "You usually roll over."

So you see, even with long-term buyers with legacy issues (my client called this a euphemism for "We always rolled over

in the past at the end of the deal to close it"), we can change
behaviors on both sides of the deal.

The customer in this situation felt the full impact of our cli-
ent's use of CNA analysis to shed light on the real alternative
and, after readjusting the power a tad, start trading. The cus-
tomer did not dislike this new approach and, in fact, seemed to
express a little more respect for this new, fact-based approach.
The customer felt reassured that the supplier was not lying or
sandbagging him, but rather was dealing with facts. As a result,
trust increased on both sides. Don't get me wrong: these deals
are still brutal, but now they're more fact-based and more bal-
anced in power and profit.

What this means in practice is that more psychological approaches
to negotiating – understanding how seats should be arranged at the
table, what different personality types will do during a negotiation
or even how culture affects who asks for what – become far less
important when you have a firm process in place for understanding
and analyzing the deal itself.

Much like CNA analysis, systematically discussing the likely terms
in the event an agreement is reached can successfully move the
focus away from price. Analyzing Levels 1, 2 and 3 negotiables, or
trades, for both sides of the deal completes the second half of your
negotiation blueprint. Armed with CNA data, trade data and a thorough analysis of both, you are now prepared to handle 97% of the
tactics that will come your way. You have also started changing the
conversation from the price of products and services to negotiating something far more valuable to both sides: solutions to business
problems.

Punch Lines:

When you're blueprinting a trade, you have to ask yourself: What are the total terms of the deal beyond price – for multiple people on both sides of the table?

CHAPTER

7

The How and Why of
Professional Buying
(And Why It's So Dangerous)

Professional Buyers Focus on Negotiation, Not Solutions

I have talked about professional buyers before, but I want to bring them up again as a way of explaining **how** price got to be such an issue, and **why** people who tell you they can "get the same thing cheaper from someone else" are often not only wrong but also dangerously mistaken, or sometimes flat-out lying.

Remember that in our SAMA study, 92% of respondents reported facing more professional buyers, such as procurement officers and senior sourcing executives, during sales negotiations. What's more, 91% of our survey respondents reported increasingly price-conscious customers, which is to be expected with the new breed of professional buyer.

While the sales professional's core competency is selling and account management, a professional buyer's core competency is negotiating. They make negotiation the issue, not the product you're pitching, the service you offer, the theme of your mission statement, the quality of your warranty or the impact of your product or service on their business. These are all variables they want to stay away from. So while you are focused on how your product or service will affect the customer organization – improving output, raising revenues, lowering TCO – the buyer is singularly focused on lowering cost (acquisition price).

What's more, professional buyers are often aided by high-powered outside consultants who plan and execute negotiation strategies based solely on reducing price and applying brutal tools like *should-cost* analysis. Meanwhile, most sellers know very little about how these professional procurement organizations function or how they are compensated.

Contrary to what buyers say, they are at least as concerned about total cost of ownership as they are about acquisition price. They know that what they're focusing on is immaterial, but they focus on it anyway just to throw you off the scent – and also because it works. For instance, suppose a buyer asks for a 10% discount, and without questioning either the rationale of the discount or the 10% figure itself, you go back to HQ asking for a 10% discount. Who wins? The buyer.

Now I think of it this way: if the buyer works for a billion dollar company and negotiates a 10% discount on a $500,000 deal, his company saved $50,000. In the larger scale of things, what percentage of overall expenses is that? .00001? .000001?

Even if buyers are not, we must be mindful of the needs of their internal customers. We need to help them focus on negotiating deals that increase revenue or improve processes that can have a much greater impact on their business than .00001% cost savings. No one gets promoted for that.

Who Professional Buyers Really Work For
(Here's a Hint: It Isn't Us!)

This is a good time to talk about for whom professional buyers actually work. No doubt you, like most salespeople reading this book, have been taught to call on multiple buying influencers who play multiple roles in a customer organization. The people you are calling on are the purchasing agent's internal customers, the people who give them the criteria for evaluating one supplier over another.

Say, for example, you are a salesperson who needs a laptop. (In truth, the buyer for your company will be sourcing laptops for the entire sales force.) Your buyer will have to speak to her internal customers:

- salespeople
- sales management
- systems department
- finance/revenue management

She asks them what their needs are and will likely hear a range of responses. Essentially, she will be scanning CNA elements, such as those listed below, in order to determine what *It* to buy and establish criteria for choosing a supplier:

- size
- weight

- remote connectivity to the Internet
- ability to integrate with other systems in the company
- speed
- reliability
- software

Next, the buyer will look at possible Level 1, 2 and 3 trades and do a trade analysis:

- Level 1: price, support costs, upgrades
- Level 2: volume, length of contract, warranty
- Level 3: joint marketing opportunities

Together, all the moving parts of the CNA and trade analyses form the true picture of this business deal. Once all of these variables are on the table simultaneously, good business decisions can be made on both sides. Of course, the alternative would be for the buyer to source the cheapest laptop available in the market. How do you think you or your team, or the IT department for that matter, would react if purchasing simply bought the cheapest machine? Not very well.

Even though this book is about negotiating, I have to tell you that selling properly, that is, selling to a buyer's internal customers, is your most effective negotiating tool. The more you know about their needs, the more you can help the buyer meet those needs, beyond just low price.

Keep the (Buyer's) Customers Satisfied

One of the major frustrations of professional buyers occurs when we effectively bias their internal customers toward our solution. Given that it's such a large frustration, I recently asked the head of purchasing for a Fortune 100 organization why he allows sellers to interact with the business people. I mean, why not simply give purchasing 100% control? His reply was that they do it because that's where all the **good, creative problem solving** happens! He was talking, of course, about Level Three trades.

This is a siren call to alert you that, when properly prepared, you are influencing the professional buyer's internal customers during the sales process. In short, you have effectively started fire prevention and begun building toward the ultimate negotiation. You negotiate what you sell, so sell well. Call on the right people at the right level selling the right thing. You won't eliminate the need for negotiating, but you will make firefighting a much more pleasant task.

How do we know this? We also consult with professional buyers at the very companies to which you sell.

This story about an airline we worked with illustrates how professional buyers work. In this instance, we had the buyer and all his internal customers in a room preparing for a multi-million dollar software negotiation to automate one of their repair depots. When we were going around the room ranking potential trades from most to least important, the professional buyer said that "price was most important." The VP of Operations literally jumped out of her chair and said, "I don't care how deep a discount you get, if it doesn't effectively automate my plant it's not worth anything!"

It was at that precise moment that I found religion for how to deal with professional buyers: understand their internal customers' needs better than they do, broaden the negotiation to include those very items and connect them to the TCO and other trades.

Just Getting the Job Done

I was facilitating a joint negotiation training session with salespeople and procurement people from the same organization. One of the sellers said (speaking to the buyers), "You know what drives me crazy? When I do all the right things and sell to the execs in my client organization, and then at the last minute they turn me over to you guys!"

The buyer looked down at the table, shook his head and smiled, as did the other buyers, before finally saying, "Do you know what happens to me in this situation? When I get the deal from one of my internal customers turned over to me, my job is to get the deal done. How does it look if I go back to that customer and say, 'You know that deal you turned over to me? Well, I screwed it up and lost it, but I'll find you another one!'"

Most salespeople hate this situation because they believe that when their deal is turned over to procurement they're screwed. But by helping them see this from the professional buyer's perspective, we can usually set them straight: being turned over to the buyer is cause for celebration, the deal is going through! Procurement's job is to get the deal done, not screw it up.

There is another helpful way of viewing the job of the professional buyer: to oversimplify a complex B2B deal. Trust me, many times they've done their homework, and in addition to knowing where you fall short in terms of, say, global infrastructure, they also *know* you have the best service in the industry and offer the longest warranty or live, 24/7 customer care. And it's not that they don't care, they just don't want you to *know* they care because it strengthens their position. Their best interests are served (or so they think) by saying that your *It* is the same as their alternative and declaring, "the only thing I care about is price."

For most of the B2B deals we work on at Think! Inc., "price" is an immense oversimplification of the total economic relationship between two firms when they agree to do business with one another. At the very least, other critical issues besides price are in play such as purchase volume, length of contract, warranty and support, not to mention loads of contract terms and conditions. A CNA analysis provides yet another dimension: how does one supplier solve our business problems better than another?

Data Keeps Sellers in Control

Both CNA and trade analyses cover most tactics that professional buyers use in negotiations. But not all buyers do these kinds of analyses, so the salesperson who does has a decided advantage. In fact, buyers who haven't done this analysis haven't properly prepared for the negotiation and, as a result, they may not completely understand their own side's position or realize what could happen if the deal falls through.

For example, a buyer believes (and behaves as if) the goods or services on the table are better, available faster or cheaper elsewhere. And remember, just because the buyer believes this doesn't make it true. If the seller hasn't done the analysis, she is likely to call HQ and say, "We've got to lower our price." This is not the road to sales greatness.

A world-class negotiator knows a buyer's CNA better than the buyer does, and they rarely, if ever, are surprised by any value claim the other side brings up in the course of the negotiation. So when a buyer throws a new item on the table late in the negotiations the seller can determine from the proper trade analysis how important the item really is and whether it's being demanded as a ruse. The seller knows how to put the new item into the proper context of the deal, diplomatically educate the buyer and refocus the conversation to the total value being negotiated.

The point is that professional buying tactics can be quite effective, but they are rendered much less so when you are armed with the facts. Sifting tactics through CNA and/or trade analysis enables you to analyze them and respond appropriately – both early and late in the negotiation. When tactics can be placed in the context of the overall deal, they can, in effect, be neutralized. I know this sounds simple, and it is, but only if you've done the proper homework.

It's not up to the professional buyer to recognize and understand all the moving parts in the deal; it's up to you. So how do you get professional buyers off the scent of price and onto the scent of matters more important to you? CNA analysis and Level 1 and Level 2 trades and, when you're ready, Level 3 trades. In the next two chapters, we'll learn how to leverage these vital tools by structuring offers that keep your customer engaged in the negotiation (in a good way) and continue to keep the focus away from price and on the value of the solutions you offer.

Punch Lines:

Selling properly, that is, selling to a buyer's internal customers, is your most effective negotiating tool.

CHAPTER

8

Problem #3:
Selling Value Then Negotiating
Products and Services

So far, so good. CNA and trade analyses have helped us move buyers away from a price-only comparison and toward the opportunity for joint value creation, ideally in exchange for price premiums or more equal risk sharing. But even if we've done a great job of creating real business value at multiple levels upstream, when it's all said and done, when all the business lunches are over and we've been awarded the contract, the customer may still say, "Ahem, you need to lower your price." So what was all the groundwork for? Why spend so much time building a foundation for value creation if it's just going to crumble once the paint dries and the dread price issue rears its ugly head?

In the traditional sales process and opportunity management scenario, professional salespeople are taught to call on multiple buyers in the client organization. They are generally very effective at uncovering client needs, then using their company's total value proposition to provide those products and services or help clients solve problems and achieve business objectives. The problem arises when all this value is positioned up front – or when the marketing department tries to communicate a company's value proposition – without finding the *It* that truly addresses this client's needs in a deal. At the back end of this negotiation, this non-specific value is all but forgotten and the actual negotiation easily slips back to being all about price.

We need a way to close this huge gap between what goes on early in the sales process and what happens near the end – after all the niceties are over and the gloves have come off – when price becomes an issue once again.

The next counterpunch, multiple equal offers (MEOs), allows you to continue to position and grow value, even late the negotiation process. By offering three different business relationships that address the needs of multiple buying influences in a way that no other competitor can, you can once and for all move the buyer's focus away from price and change the nature of the conversation and client relationship for good.

9

Counterpunch #3:
Multiple Equal Offers

I'd like to invite you to a fancy restaurant tonight. But this is not just any fancy restaurant. It is the type of restaurant you read about in the tabloids because celebrities are always there. It's the kind of place you normally have to book at least six months in advance. It's the kind of place with three-hour waits and long lines at the valet stand as the paparazzi peer around to look at someone famous inside. Now, this restaurant doesn't have a fancy name, but I'm sure you'll recognize it; it's called the Fixed Price Negotiation.

Funny thing about this place, there's not a lot of variety. In fact, when you walk through the front door, the maître d' grabs you by the scruff of the neck and shoves you toward the worst table in the joint. He sits you down and says, "This is where you're going to sit," no ifs, ands or buts; no discussion about window seats or booths versus tables. Then he whips out a menu, points to a meal you may or may not want and says, "This is what you're going to eat," forget the fish of the day, the soup du jour or the chef's special. Then he closes the menu before you can even see the price and leans down to whisper in your ear, "This is how much it's going to cost."

That doesn't sound so appealing, does it? So let me invite you to another restaurant where there are no lines and you're always the most famous person in the joint. Here you get to sit wherever you want: by the window, in a cozy booth for two in the corner or at a special table in front of the open kitchen line. You have a variety of menu items and, what's more, you can select them based on quantity, taste or price.

"What's the name of this great place?" you ask. It's called **multiple equal offers (MEOs)**, *which also happens to be the name of B2B Street Fighting's* **counterpunch #3**.

We use MEOs to shift perspective from one fixed-price offer for your products and services to a choice of different business relationships, each of which focuses on value and problem solving in a slightly different way. So instead of showing up with a hard, firm line in the sand with a fixed price wrought from thoughtful trading, you show up with three MEOs that are equal in value to you, but vary in value to the customer or, more accurately, to different influencers in the customer organization.

On the surface, this flies in the face of traditional negotiating advice, which discourages such behavior for fear of muddying the waters. But what's the alternative? The Fixed Price Negotiation (and none of us wants to eat there again). At the Fixed Price Negotiation, you sit down at the bargaining table, shove a sheet of paper across the table, sit back, fold your arms and say, "Here's our offer." Ouch. What does *that* accomplish? It immediately sets up a competitive atmosphere and, mathematically speaking, a zero-sum situation. In fact, you could even say it begs the question, "do you think you can get this cheaper elsewhere?"

> *Have you been to a fast-food drive-through lately? If you have, you probably noticed more choices than were there a year or two ago. Now, instead of just being able to get fries and a soda with your burger, you have a wide variety of menu items to choose from. So you could, theoretically, drive away with the traditional burger, fries and a soda, or you could enjoy a broiled chicken sandwich, side salad and unsweetened tea. You might even drive off with a soy burger, unsalted pretzels and apple juice.*
>
> *MEOs are a lot like the fast food place; everyone leaves with a full belly, but it doesn't necessarily have to be filled with the same food.*

MEOs makes negotiation significantly more collaborative by moving everyone involved to the same side of the table. They work because they offer true variety – burger or soy, fries or fresh fruit, soda or juice – not just the illusion of variety. They live up to their name because they are not just variations on a theme that obscure fixed price negotiation with smoke and mirrors.

MEOs help you combat the disconnect between **selling value and then negotiating prices of products and services** by enabling you to come to the table prepared with something for everybody. Your thorough analysis of the real facts of the deal combined with knowing what all the influencers need from this deal makes you the only seller capable of offering the customer exactly what they need. Your offers and the value they represent can no longer be compared to those from "someone else."

Your competitors either lose out immediately with their stubborn insistence on dining at the Fixed Price Negotiation or, at the opposite end of the spectrum, with their giveaways of the farm because they're unprepared or have no formal negotiation strategy. Meanwhile you can serenely present three MEOs that make the buyers on the other side of the table feel like you are willing to go the distance.

So what business problem does this solve? Let's revisit our favorite sentence one last time, shall we? "I can get the same thing (commoditization pressure) cheaper (price focus) from someone else (selling value then negotiating prices of products and services)."

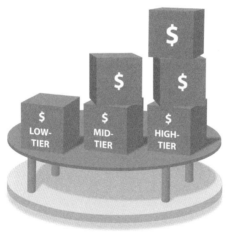

MEOs

Designing MEOs

It's imperative to use thoughtful, well researched CNA and trade analyses when preparing and presenting MEOs. A complete CNA analysis takes the pressure off commoditization and helps both sides agree on what's really being sold (i.e., the one, two or perhaps three things that differentiate you from the competition, given the client's needs in this deal). Trade analysis gets all the moving parts on the table so you can determine what the ideal terms look like for both buyer and seller. Now we can use that information to build strong MEOs tailored for this deal; CNA analysis helps you title them and trade analysis helps you populate them.

It's also crucial to take into consideration the needs of multiple buying influencers at the buyer's company. This means working upstream and preparing carefully to create three offers that, if designed specifically for the client in question, can change the conversation for good from the price of your products to the value of your solutions.

Let's get started. When deciding what to include in each offer, start by asking yourself: *What does a great deal look like for both sides?* Now consider the following:

- Look back at your CNA analysis, at the two or three things that differentiate you in this deal, ways in which you solve this customer's problems better. Use the gap between your offer and the competition's to identify the theme for at least one or two of your MEOs.

- Design three offers of equal value to you, but that vary in value to different influencers in the customer organization.

- Think carefully about how you will name each MEO. This is not just about wording titles for a slide; how you name MEOs is key. In fact, selecting (and then presenting) MEO titles is the next most important task after the prep work that goes into building them. Naming is often a good place to start developing MEOs since it helps establish the business goal, customer appeal or product alternatives you're structuring in this offer.

  For naming inspiration refer back to those two or three items you chose from your pick box, your *It* in this deal. You can also draw an MEO's name from the collection of trades embedded in a particular offer, from the way it meets the customer's needs or by the risk balancing this MEO is designed to accomplish.

Use customer language that punches a point of value *and* exploits your strength. Think of each name as a statement of "solution," something for which the customer has been searching or something you know they will need. One of the worst things you can do is name an MEO based on "high, medium or low price" or as "A, B or C" since they offer no description and hold no appeal for the customer.

MEO titles can effectively change the conversation and the entire nature of the expectations game from one of zero-sum pricing discussions to a value-creating business relationship. Let me show you why, using an example from our workshops where we create 100% custom case studies for participants to use in practicing negotiations.

Think! was working on a deal to land a potential client after its merger with another technology company. We knew that the client's CNA, our closest competitor, was likely to use generic business school case studies in their training class, so we used this knowledge to our advantage. We titled one MEO "negotiating in a post-merger world."

In this relationship, we punched hard with what we had that the alternative didn't, custom cases designed to have the staff practicing negotiation in the post-merger environment with "rubber bullets." To accomplish that, we wrote case studies that reflected what their buyers were likely to do, which is to default to price (i.e., "I used to buy $1 million from each of you; now I'm buying $2 million from one of you, so I expect twice the discount.")

*It's likely that we saved the client millions by preparing their team for this realistic scenario; no business school case studies could have done that. We punched our **It** hard simply by how we titled our MEOs.*

Many of us were taught in the old days that we should up-sell our own value, not pick apart the competition. We say, "Bull feathers!" You *absolutely* need to punch why you're different or better, in a diplomatic way of course, to help the client make better business decisions.

- Bundle into each offer the combination of trades that best solves this customer's business problems – the way you have described in its title. The various elements within one MEO should all be interdependent, designed to balance what you "give" with what you want in return. Later, when you're presenting these offers, this makes it much harder for a customer to focus only on price, since price is set based on other components of the offer – volume, length of contract, warranties, etc. It can't be changed out of context of the other variables in this MEO.

- Nearly every trade has either underlying risk or reward. When this is true, one of your goals is to build MEOs that differ in the way they allow buyer and seller to balance risk and reward. For example, one offer might require a larger up-front prepayment while the other spreads payments over time.

- Each MEO is designed to offer a different relationship or solution, so the three MEOs themselves should be interdependent. I'll talk more about this shortly.

Present Your MEOs Then Get Ready for *More* Trading

Initial MEOs in hand, the entire process comes alive when you present them to the client. You want as many buying influencers as possible present at this meeting, whether you meet online or face-to-face. (Remember back in the old days when people used to travel?)

Here, it's important to follow specific steps in a specific order. The more effectively each step is executed, the better the final presentation will be.

1. **Review MEO titles**

   First go over all of the MEO titles without going into the trades. Remember that the titles were carefully chosen to be succinct descriptions of the customer's options, the risk sharing, the problems solved, etc. Don't provide too much information too fast or you'll risk presenting multiple "confusing" offers. Tell a brief story about each of the three MEOs by elaborating on their titles and the relationship being presented by each.

Focus on how each offer solves the client's business problems and is different from the alternative's offers.

2. **Review key trades in each offer**

Next, overview the key trades in each offer. Highlight the essence of the differences between each offer. Don't review all the trades, as there might be 20 or more for all three levels.

For example, when we recently presented MEOs to a large tech firm, two key trades involved either up-front payment for use of our intellectual property (IP) or a per-person fee for use over time. There were many other trades in the MEOs, but these were the key ones.

These alternatives enabled each party to choose the risk/ reward they preferred: if they paid us up front, say $100,000 for use of our IP for five years, they assumed more risk in the event they didn't actually use the IP broadly in their organiza-tion. (We did offer to discount those fees to compensate for that risk.) The other choice was to pay us on a per-person basis for five years, which lowered their risk of a big cash payout but raised the risk of paying out 40% more over time, based on the total expected audience for our IP. Their risk from a big up-front payout was lower and, in effect, we paid ourselves back for assuming the risk of per-person fees over time.

These kinds of trades are the heart and soul of almost every B2B deal. We like to think of contingent contract trades when there is uncertainty about the future, which in this case was about how many people were going to use the IP. We simply put a bet in place that said, "if this, then that"; each side can bet on its version of the future.

Different offers are also a great way to share or balance risk and reward between two parties with different views. For instance, let's say a customer believes the price of raw mate-rials will go up, and you believe they will go down. Well, neither of you has a crazy aunt with a crystal ball, so you design two MEOs that lets one side bet on the price of raw materials going up, and the other side bet on the price going down. Whoever is right wins.

3. **Ask the customer to rank the MEOs**

   Ask the members of the audience to rank the three offers in terms of their preference.

4. **Rearrange**

   Next, rearrange the MEOs based on the customer's rankings. Why? Well, the client rarely accepts any of the MEOs in the first round. MEO reorganization usually results in a complete re-thinking of the offers followed by a second round of presentations. This is normal, as the first meeting educates the client and gives you a sense of what's most-to-least important. It also begins to change the conversation ... which is *exactly* what you want.

   We tend to think of the first round of presentations as the opportunity to accomplish the following tasks:

   - Changing the conversation from the price of products to the value of solutions and the underlying risks and rewards for both sides
   - Broadening the negotiation from a single zero-sum issue to multiple items that can be traded further, much like the dog shampoo and rent offset in my earlier anecdote
   - Differentiating you from virtually every other offer the buyer will see
   - Allowing you to effectively conduct a sensitivity analysis meeting and take control of the negotiation by educating the clients on all the moving parts of the larger deal. This task is important because you are probably sitting in a room with clients who have not thought through any CNA and trades analyses.

   Rearranging the MEOs is an especially valuable tool for dealing with professional buyers who want the lowest price.

You often offer a low-price MEO that leaves out many of the items that their internal customers wanted in the deal. What typically happens is that the offer misses the mark by such a wide margin that the buyer can clearly see that getting the price they want means **not** meeting the needs of their internal customers.

Bring Your Total Value Back Into Context

these parts are all interdependent, not independent

investments and risks (trades)	what the customer is buying (CNA)
• price	• global infrastructure
• service and support	• customization
• length of contract	• ease of implementation
• volume	• integration
• etc.	• etc.

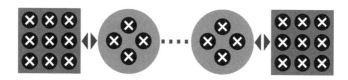

Trades within each MEO and the three MEOs themselves are all interdependent.

Deals Are Interdependent Wildlife Ecosystems

It's important to remember that the various elements within one MEO are all interdependent. So if a customer wants to focus only on the price element, you can't because that price is set based on the volume, length of contract, warranties, etc., which are all part of that offer. If you tinker with one item in an offer, you impact all the others. Sometimes it's helpful to think of the multiple data points of a deal (CNA/trade) as an interdependent wildlife ecosystem. What you do to one species affects every other.

For instance, killing off the white owl might not seem too tragic (unless you're a white owl) until you recognize that the mouse population will now triple and overtake another part of

*the ecosystem. The mice gobble up their favorite prey, the forest
mosquito, whose typical prey, the red ant, now thrives because
the forest mosquitoes are gone. The red ants eat all the cherry
blossoms, which then cost the lives of the gossamer butterflies,
who in turn aren't around to feed on the... get the picture?*

Deals are like that. If you mess with a price that is based on the
It you're selling that is tied into volume, length of contract, etc., you
are upsetting the balance of the ecosystem. Who knows what other
part of the deal you might kill off in the process?

You can nonetheless expect that buyers will try to cherry pick
the deal or ask for the highest value offer at the lowest price. Your
response should be automatic: as soon as someone tinkers with one
aspect of an offer, all the items in that offer are up for discussion!

MEOs Can Bridge the Accuracy Gap in Your Data

Even after you've completed deep-dive CNA and trade analyses for
multiple players on both sides of the deal, your research might be
only 50% accurate, especially when you first start out (later your hit
rate goes up). But even then, you still probably have 80% to 90%
more real data than you've had in the past!

MEOs can help bridge that accuracy gap. When you put three
value-creating solutions to the customer's real problems on the table,
you start an interdependent dialogue with multiple players on both
sides of the deal. This dialogue will likely pull out the last few pieces
of data. Very infrequently does any customer or group of buying
influencers take one of your three offers the first time they're on the
table; but the offers do shift the negotiation in a fairly radical way – to
everyone's benefit except the competition's!

MEOs: The Swiss Army Knife of Negotiation

One final note: MEOs work on small pop-up negotiations with
existing customers as well as on large, complex deals with global
customers. Heck, I even use them on my kids! I say, "Okay, you have
three choices:"

1. "Good grades and you can go to skateboarding camp."
2. "Bad grades and no camp."
3. "Average grades and you pay for half of camp."

This tool also works with request for proposal (RFP) responses. If you get an RFP or a request for a quote (RFQ), respond as you are asked. Answer the questions exactly, but add in one or two more offers based on your analysis of what this customer may want or need.

The first time I heard of "MEOs" was during a discussion with my business partner, Max, after our first year in business together. We had a profitable year – not spectacular, but adequate. I looked at how that profit was divided and noticed that Max received more. In short, he had basically out-negotiated me (without cleaning my clock). No surprise there; after all, he is the source of all that is good in negotiating, and I am merely the proud blue-collar son of a barkeep. I was too intimidated to renegotiate with His Maxness, but I invited him to lunch. After kibitzing for a bit, I blurted out, "Max, I'm not making enough money here!"

*In response, he leaned back in his chair, stroked his professorial beard and replied, "So you want some of mine." I nearly fell out of my chair! I had just broken a cardinal rule of negotiating: **never negotiate one thing**. Instead, I should have brought the natural robustness of a business deal to the table, so there could be trading. (I should have done a CNA analysis, for crying out loud!) In fact, if we hadn't reached agreement then, I would have had to go back and get a real job and Max would have continued teaching. (We see who had more power in this deal.)*

Max then did something really cool. He asked me to consider one of three offers:

1. He takes more cash flow and trades me some of his equity, or
2. He accepts less cash flow and takes some of my equity, or
3. Perhaps there is not enough money here, and we dissolve the firm.

Dang it, he did CNA analysis and used the third MEO to let me know that he knew that my CNA was to get a J-O-B. Not even an option for me; I love what I do too much. So I threw out that option. He then asked me which of the two remaining options offended me least. (I swear he did!)

I said #1, which was strange since I came there looking for money. What he had done was also expand the trade beyond a single-item, zero-sum deal by adding in equity.

Then he said, "So you value long-term equity more than short-term cash flow?"

I said, "Yes, in fact, I do. But I didn't realize it until you just played this little game with me. What the hell did you just do?"

He said, "I just gave you multiple equal offers."

In other words, he had used my CNA and developed trades that moved a one-item, single-issue, win/lose negotiation to creation of a value deal that was better than my CNA. In fact, what I found out later was that he was moving from Kellogg Business School in Evanston, Illinois, to Harvard University in Cambridge, Massachusetts, and needed more cash flow for the move, exactly the thing I was asking from him.

I truly believe that if he hadn't done this, we would have come to an impasse – emotionally speaking – over money, you wouldn't be reading this book and I would have a "real" job somewhere else. The other thing Max did was use these offers as a sensitivity analysis for my needs in the deal. He learned that I value long-term equity and that I felt more confident that I was going to run the business the right way.

CNA, trading, MEOs – it all goes back to breaking free of fire-fighter and moving target mentalities. All businesses are trained to sell value. What is the total solution my company provides? What problems are solved by buying my product? But what good is it if we sell value only to negotiate low price on the back end?

As B2B street fighters, we are in a unique position to resolve this situation. We can firefight if need be, as MEOs are very effective fire-fighting tools (they keep disparate pieces of the deal in context of the broader deal). But these tools are about fire prevention, using CNA and trade analyses to prepare and present MEOs. This means working upstream and preparing carefully to create three offers that, if designed specifically for the client in question, can change the conversation from the prices of your products to the value of your solutions.

MEOs help you continue to create value to the end. Presenting three different business solutions to customer problems is a way to build relationships without burning bridges or sending everyone to eat at The Fixed Price Negotiation!

Punch Lines:

MEOs help you change the conversation from the price of products to the value of solutions, given the customer's needs and their alternative to reaching agreement with you.

CHAPTER

10

Negotiating Like a B2B Street Fighter: Quick Review

Good news, you're almost ready for battle! Now, let's take one last walk through a typical negotiation using our three counterpunches. For all three steps, it helps to think of multiple stakeholders on both the buy and sell sides to create that natural complexity or robustness I've been talking about.

Our research showed us that 97% of verbal tactics are intended to accomplish one or two things:

- reference an alternative to doing business with you
- leverage this alternative to bargain

51% of tactics correlate with both alternatives and concessions. These tactics sound something like, "I can get the same thing cheaper," but we hear it expressed in many ways, with different words and different emotions. For tactics related to alternatives, CNA analysis helps change the conversation to something like this.

Q: *"Your competition has better global infrastructure than you."*
A: *"How important is that compared to other items we've discussed?"*

46% of tactics correlate with leverage only, resembling something like "lower your price," or "my budget is only x amount of $." Here, trading analysis changes the dialogue so something like this.

Q: *"You need to lower your price."*
A: *"There might be a pathway to that, can we talk about length of contract, volume or terms?"*

Our scary sentence, "I can get the same thing cheaper from someone else," helped us capture in a succinct way the three biggest problems embedded in typical buyer tactics of both kinds so we could tackle them one at a time.

"The same thing" and tactics like it let buyers clearly establish that they view this transaction like a commodity buy, where products are differentiated only by price. To neutralize commoditization pressure, **consequence of no agreement (CNA) analysis** lets you change the conversation about "alternatives" to an apples-to-apples comparison of what's really being sold.

"Cheaper" and it's friends "lower price" and "10% discount" are every buyers mantra at virtually every step of a negotiation. To handle this never-ending price pressure, **trade analysis** helps you move the focus away from price to a more productive discussion about the total terms of the deal.

"From someone else" is never what you want to hear once you've spent months selling value. To keep you from reverting to a price-based negotiation after successfully selling value upstream, **multiple equal offers (MEOs)** help you tailor a deal that optimizes customer value – for the buyer and all his internal customers – and gives you price premiums for the value you offer.

With CNA and trade data ready and MEOs prepared, you can take control of the conversation, change the relationship and build value for everyone. Now, let's review those moves one more time before we take this fight to the streets.

Step #1: Your first counterpunch for combating commoditization pressure is CNA analysis. It helps you get the facts about the client's real alternative to you, as well as the facts about all aspects of your value proposition on the table.

Why is this necessary? People tend to take a deal when it is better than the alternative. People also view offers as a plus or a minus according to how they perceive the alternative. Ultimately, showing the customer how your deal meets their needs better (not cheaper) than their CNA is how everyone gets to win-win. Overall, the result is better decisions by all parties, so both sides end up with something better than the alternative. This is also the first step in creating value.

Step #2: Counterpunch #2 (trading or trading analysis) helps you combat price pressure by collecting *all* the facts about all the terms that need to be agreed upon, in addition to price, then trading those things to provide more value than they cost (like working up those cool trades I talked about with Maxine).

Remember that trades are a method of designing a deal in which everybody gets something equally valuable. In publishing, the book is never really finished until all the rewrites have been done and both the publisher and the author agree the book is in the best possible form. Trades are the rewriting you do at the bargaining table.

Step #3: Finally, counterpunch #3 helps you avoid the problem of selling value then reverting back to negotiating price by "packaging" the value created during trading analysis into three unique MEOs. These MEOs describe three different business relationships – often targeting the priorities of different buying influencers – that exceed both sides' CNA and trade analyses on as many items as possible.

MEOs keep the value expansion going and help you keep the focus off of price. I often use this explanation because it ties the concept of *how* to the goal of *what*. We also point out in our workshops that if you pursue this goal, there will be a radical shift in how you act as a negotiator. Buyers on the other side will also need to be re-educated because of their self-limiting beliefs about what negotiation really is.

I know, I know! You *still* don't believe that it can really be that simple. But it is! I'll tell you what I tell my customers: "Don't trust me on this three counterpunches thing just yet. Let me prove it." After a quick pre-fight check in the next chapter, we'll put our counterpunches to the test.

Punch Lines:

With CNA and trade data ready and MEOs prepared, you can take control of the conversation, change the relationship, and build value for everyone.

CHAPTER

11

You Can Be Trained to Expect the Unexpected

The ultimate goals for any negotiation are to *create joint value* and to *divide that value given concerns for fairness in the ongoing relationship*. At Think!, we've made it our mission to completely redefine how our customers think about the negotiation process to accomplish these goals. And yet we know there is no quick fix for the far-reaching and frankly quite challenging problems of modern negotiation.

You are reading this book because you're tired of sinking months and sometimes years of work into tough deals, trying to give the buyer what you think she wants, then ultimately losing because nothing happened the way you thought it would. At the least, I hope you are here to find a way to avoid the pain of repeating this experience again. You know what they say about the definition of insanity … it's doing the same thing you've always done and expecting a different outcome.

If this book has accomplished one thing, it is to convince you that you can, indeed, predict and prepare for what buyers are doing and fight back. In the next chapter we'll work through a real negotiation using our three counterpunches. Before we get started, let's go through a "pre-fight" check to warm up your street fighter and get into a fighting, winning mindset.

First, we need a winning attitude aligned to combating buyer tactics differently than you have in the past. Despite your experiences, you can anticipate what may and probably will happen in negotiation, so let's start preparing.

Remember Who Your Opponent Really Is

In the end, the problem is not that the buyer is saying tough things such as "I can get the same thing cheaper from someone else," nor is the solution learning how to say even tougher things back. In fact, the problem was never with the buyer at all.

You are not and should not be fighting your customers. We make money by negotiating *with* them, and they use our valuable assets to solve problems in their companies. The challenge is with not knowing enough – about your company and what it offers, about the competition and what they offer or about the total economic scope of the deal – so you can proceed with confidence and skill.

The real "street fight" is with the buyer's alternative to us (CNA). We are just geeky, rational, fact-based street fighters working on behalf of our company *and* our customers. The most common problem, simply stated, usually comes from a lack of data:

1. Not knowing enough about the *Its* that you and the competitor are offering
2. Not recognizing all the trades that exist within the deal, outside of price
3. Not preparing three offers

The solution is collecting or using better data in three key areas: collecting and analyzing CNA data; collecting and analyzing trade data; and MEOs, an amazingly lethal (competitively speaking) way to present the data and analysis results.

Bigger Pies Mean Bigger Pie Pieces

If you want to build value-based, collaborative relationships with buyers, every negotiation is a good opportunity to practice. And if you want to work with this company in the future, don't set out to take advantage of them or take cheap shots in fighting language.

Most people (especially tough, old-school buyers) think of negotiation as a pie-eating contest; that is, they want to get as much as they can to win the prize and screw the other guy. This is an extremely near-sighted strategy that may work in the short term, but these buyers will always be looking for new customers because they've burned so many bridges.

Conversely, *real* negotiation is about making the pie, and thus the pie pieces, bigger. You need to go in thinking about both the competitive and cooperative aspects of working together to create more value for both sides (as I did with Maxine, the dog groomer). And the three-step blueprinting process you just learned – CNA, trades and

MEOs – lets you achieve this with clients while being ruthless with your competitors.

Most of us have been taught that we get ahead by up-selling our own value, not by attacking the competition. I say you need to be ruthless about the competition; this is what CNA analysis is all about: tearing apart the competitor's value from the perspective of multiple buyer influences and then presenting that data in a way that benefits multiple buyers (i.e., MEOs).

This philosophy has never been more appropriate than it is today, during one of the worst economies since the Great Depression. Now more than ever, it's either an all-out fight for shrinking margins or a redefinition of how two firms negotiate based on the facts.

Negotiations Are Predictable, Problems Are Resolvable

Sometimes when you're solving a problem, your assumptions are flawed or out-of-date, so problem solving suffers. If you assume negotiation is unpredictable, you will be more likely to lose control and lose the deal when the unexpected happens *because* you approached the problem as unpredictable.

But now we know that negotiation follows patterns that, say it with me, "are predictable." In the past, "getting it elsewhere cheaper" might have scared the crap out of you, but now you know to expect this and know what to do about it.

For example, let's say I took Maxine's request to take $50 off of her rent at face value and balked, refusing to even consider all the other variables we could trade to reach a mutually satisfying conclusion. I'd be out a dog groomer/walker/sitter in my apartment building and the $235 of value we created in the negotiation.

Many people would have refused Maxine's offer outright – or any counteroffer for that matter – for a variety of reasons. Perhaps it wasn't in their script, or they panicked because it wasn't the rigid Fixed Price Negotiation to which they were accustomed. Whatever the reason, if you look at negotiation as an uncontrollable, five-alarm-fire scenario, you will never truly approach it from a creative problem-solving perspective and remain in control, ultimately creating the most value for all parties.

Even after you've carefully prepared, after you've thrown your three counterpunches, I can guarantee that the customer will say certain things, chief among them: "lower your price," "you are difficult," etc. When this happens, it's easy to fall back to the assumption that you can't predict what the other side will say or do next. But now you know you can.

Three Counterpunches Knockout 97% of Buyer Tactics

When you understand and master *B2B Street Fighting's* three counterpunches, you can control the uncontrollable and expect the unexpected. This flies in the face of how virtually every negotiation writer and consultant thinks about the art. For example, a distinguished professor at Kellogg Business School at Northwestern University has written a book entitled *The Truth About Negotiation* (FT Press, 2007) that reveals what the author refers to as 53 Negotiation Truths.

How do we as individual negotiators prepare for 53 truths? How do companies try to install corporate negotiation competency around 53 truths? But it doesn't stop there. Recently we saw an ad in *Selling Power* magazine for a report about negotiation training. It included:

- Five lessons
- Nine important ways to prepare
- Seven key behaviors
- Twelve predictions

Okay, so there's less to memorize here than 53 responses, but we ask the same question: How does an individual or an organization optimize and adopt 33 items? Our response is simple: they don't.

We know that 97% of buyers' verbal tactics can be **anticipated** and **prepared for**. Almost everything you're going to hear is tied to defining *It*, agreeing on what the customer will pay for *It* and what you will accept for *It*.

Negotiation really can be this systematic and simple *if* you are willing to collect the right data and prepare. Thorough answers to these two questions will assist you in doing just that:

1. What are the total consequences to both sides if we don't agree?
2. What are the total terms of the deal in the event we do agree?

CNA Analysis Keeps the Details in Context

Often we negotiate things out of context. Gathering all the facts around a coherent CNA analysis helps you have a more collaborative, apples-to-apples discussion about what's being sold and starts the process of getting all the relevant trades (not just price) on the table. This effectively combats dealmakers who approach negotiation as a random series of jabs rather than as a rational business process.

For instance, in one of my first examples, the e-learning company was focusing on price out of context. They were worried they weren't offering as much as their competitors based on price or content alone. But when I got them to step back and look at price in context with everything else they were offering – 43 hard and measurable items that could be personalized for the buyer on a deal-by-deal basis – they could see just how valuable their company was.

Now sometimes when you analyze your company relative to your competitor, the statement, "I can get the same thing cheaper from someone else," will be true. If you analyze the trades, brainstorm your differences and *still* come up short, that's a value proposition problem for your firm that requires more than simply sitting down at the bargaining table. You have to look farther upstream and figure out *why* you're not providing as much value for your clients as your competition, then rectify the situation internally.

Now It's Your Fight to Lose

As a B2B street fighter, it's your job to get the negotiation process back on track by getting more facts on the table and literally steering the fight where you want it to go. In other words, you want to start proactively managing the deal versus thinking about negotiation as a tactical response to a professional buyer. It's all about acting first, not reacting later. With the three counterpunches you've learned, you should no longer be thinking, "S-O-S! S-O-S! I've got to get my ship out of these stormy waters and live to fight another day!" Instead, you start thinking, "I'm going to be steering the ship into calmer seas, where I can get a better perspective, make a better deal for me and provide a better solution for my customer." Now you can approach any deal from an aspect of preparedness and partnership. You know to come bearing three equal offers, and you know you're not going to a pie-eating contest! Now this street fight is yours to win or lose.

They're Called "Professional" Buyers for a Reason

Professional buyers say the things they do and demand zero-sum concessions because it's their job, because the sales world allows it, and because these tactics work! It's time to put an end to this.

Fair warning: this takes practice. Buyers are skilled at extracting pieces of a larger negotiation, particularly but not exclusively price, and using them out of context. It's the job of the B2B street fighter to bring all the moving parts of a negotiation to the table. This can only be accomplished by systematically collecting data on the negotiation **before the actual event**. This whole three-step approach we call *fire prevention* or *blueprinting* will go a long way – in fact 97% of the way – toward helping you to stop reacting to your customers' demands and start taking proactive control of your negotiation outcome.

Turn Tactics into Trades

Negotiation should never be approached as a fire sale, where, for example, there's always a deadline looming or some stubborn price point the customer must have: "I want to close it next week," "I want to close it for this price point," or "I need this percentage." These are not goals, but merely tactics. In fact, closing by a certain date is a trade and perhaps an important one, and shouldn't be an overall end goal for the dealmaker. Similarly, obtaining a certain price point is also a trade. When you set a buyer tactic like one of these as a goal, instead of viewing it as the trading opportunity it presents, it ultimately sub-optimizes your deals. Bottom line, you have a higher chance of reaching a goal if you set one, so set it carefully. If your goal is "closing the deal by next week," you're likely to hit it, often at the expense of the value and or price premiums left behind.

"Same thing cheaper" Is a Myth

And finally, I hope this book has helped to blow away two common myths:

1. "I can get the same thing cheaper."
2. "Negotiations are a moving target; you never know what's going to happen."

Now you know that your customer most likely can't get the same thing cheaper, and negotiations are not moving targets. We *can* know (almost) everything that is going to happen in most B2B negotiations. Good data empowers sellers to counter typical buyer tactics and to know in advance what is likely to happen. We can no longer be intellectually lazy about business negotiation by putting the blame on something as subjective or esoteric as "it's unpredictable."

By now, "I can get the same thing cheaper from someone else" seems pretty tame, doesn't it? Well, that's because we've picked it apart, examined it inch-by-inch and put it back together again so that it's not so scary.

How did we do that? We analyzed it according to the three key problems you face in your day-to-day business and offered a solution using success-breeding secrets. "I can get the same thing (**commoditization pressure/CNA**) cheaper (**price pressure/trading**) from someone else." Then we offered the ultimate solution for *keeping* the conversation focused on the value of your solutions while making you the only seller who can deliver them using **MEOs**.

When you understand and behave as if negotiation is neither a moving target nor unpredictable, it changes the rules of the game.

Negotiation is, and always has been, about one thing: data, data and more data. Data on the *It* that's being negotiated and data on what both sides will pay/accept for *It*.

When you take the time to prepare strong data, the tired tactics used by professional buyers are virtually useless. In the words of one Think! Inc. consultant, "we have to change the conversation with the customer, and it is only with the right data that this can be done effectively." Now let's hit the streets and break in our new moves!

Punch Lines:

We have to change the conversation with the customer, and it is only with the right data that this can be done effectively.

CHAPTER

12

Using the Blueprinting Process in a Large and Complex Negotiation

Our three counterpunches – CNA analysis, trade analysis and MEOs – have worked for virtually every large and small deal I've done anywhere in the world. The only thing that changes is the number of variables in the analyses and, ultimately, the complexity of the MEOs.

For pages, you've been reading about what they can do for you. Now it's time for the rubber to meet the road. Let's try out our process on a live deal. This exercise involves thorough analysis and effective customer questioning around three aspects of the negotiation blueprint.

It's important to note here that while this book has introduced the counterpunches in logical 1-2-3 order, in real negotiations the blueprinting process proceeds in a more iterative fashion. When you start collecting data and analyzing the deal, more possibilities open up and some avenues close. You collect data, rough out trades, present MEOs, get more data, retool better trades, and so on, sometimes even going back and revisiting CNA assumptions. This is the reality of real negotiation. In our simplified example here, the three counterpunches are used in the order that makes sense for this deal.

It's April 1st and you've just been told by a potential new global customer that after all your months of trying to sell some of your machines to them, it's finally down to a choice between you and your closest competitor. The customer wants to see your best-foot-forward proposal by May 15th (six weeks). He has hinted that your competitor is aggressively pursuing the business, is being quite creative on price and has a pretty good product fit.

At this point in this negotiation, you have already completed your pick box to determine your company's value proposition. So first, we do a CNA analysis to determine the *It* relative to this deal.

Complete Your CNA

Start by asking yourself: what are the consequences to my company of not closing this deal?

You determine that if you don't reach agreement with the customer in this negotiation you will most likely lose the business, which in this case is a loss of about $750K in global revenue in the first year in addition to potential long-term revenues, totaling up to $2.5M. In addition, you will lose the costs associated with the four months you've spent selling to the customer – approximately $25K for staff time, product demonstrations, etc.

You will also have some soft costs in the form of political heat from your Vice President of Global Sales and the head of your product management group, both of whom have a personal interest in this sale as it impacts their bonuses, as well as yours. And of course, losing this sale will send revenues to a competitor.

The good news for your CNA is that the market is growing – albeit slowly compared to previous years. The chances of replacing this customer are fairly good and your list of other sales prospects looks good at the moment. Also, while you have no other customers that are this large and ready to close, there are at least two or three smaller ones about which you feel positive. All of them together could replace this sale, but it's always more profitable to close and service one customer than several.

Complete Your Customer's CNA

Start by asking yourself: what are the consequences to the customer of not closing this deal with me? It's sometimes helpful to reframe this question; how will the customer meet his needs in this deal if he does not close this deal with me?

As always, attempting to identify the customer's CNA is trickier. In this case, you know they will go to your major competitor and, as they've hinted, pay less. What's tricky, though, is the total analysis – that is, determining the positive and negative effects – of their choosing the competitor over you.

First, you pull together a team from your side. You invite one of the company's account managers who worked for your competitor on this deal, a guy from engineering who just came to you from the customer's organization and some additional product experts. You give them an overview of the situation and ask them to help you brainstorm all the elements the customer may be considering when comparing your offer to their CNA.

After brainstorming you ask the group whether, from the customer's perspective, each element is positive or negative compared to choosing you. The team breaks down the analysis in terms of the design of the solution, delivery and installation, ongoing maintenance, output and long-term upkeep. They also suggest doing an evaluation of comparative terms and conditions.

The results of their analysis suggest that the following questions must be addressed:

Design Elements

- Is there is an off-the-shelf solution that fits the customer's needs?
- How much ground-up design is needed to build and test custom features?
- How much time/commitment is needed from the customer for design?

Delivery and Installation Elements

- How long will it take?
- How long will the customer's operation be down while the machine is being installed?
- How labor intensive will it be for the customer?

Maintenance Elements

- How often does the machine break down?
- What are the service hours and fees?
- How difficult will it be to train the customer's team to run it?

Output Elements

- How many units per hour will the machine put out?
- What is the defect rate of the customer's machine?
- Can the machine be run 24/7?

Upkeep Elements

- What do maintenance costs look like in years two, three and four?
- How easy is the machine to upgrade?
- What is the machine's expected service life?

Terms and Conditions Elements

- Lease vs. buy
- Flexibility of contracts
- Payment terms
- Short-term product price

Now, you consider each group of questions relative to your competitor. In regard to *design*, you've determined that your competitor does have a pretty good off-the-shelf machine, while yours would require some customization. Your customization, however, would be free, and would require very little customer interface.

In terms of *installation*, your engineering department has just found some independent studies showing that easily customizable machines – like yours – are also relatively easy to install, and therefore end up taking about the same total time to install as less flexible, off-the-shelf machines.

As far as *maintenance* is concerned, the folks in your engineering department, and especially the engineer that just came over from the customer, say you have a huge advantage in terms of your machine's reliability. Of course, customers aren't likely to tell you that, but it's one of your strengths.

In regard to *output*, you and your competitor are pretty close. Their output may be a bit higher than yours, but your machines run a higher percentage of the time, which will probably make up for the difference.

In terms of *upkeep*, because of how they've been engineered, your machines break down much less frequently and, as a result, last longer.

Finally, in regard to *terms and conditions*, you and your competitor both offer lease or buy options. Your industry contracts are all pretty much the same and payment terms are usually 25% at signing, 25% on delivery and 50% when running. Your price is a bit higher, but you've determined that because of the reliability and flexibility of your machines they have less downtime, easier long-term upgrades and a longer shelf life. As a result, not only does the ROI from your machines get better after year one, they are also less expensive to own in years two and three.

In answering the questions about each group of elements, you've determined that there is a value proposition gap between what you have to offer and the customer's CNA (your competitor) in all but one of them: output. Based on that, you feel good about this negotiation; however, the problem is that either your buyer doesn't have all the data on his CNA that you do, or he's bluffing.

Blueprint the Trades for Both Sides

Prepare Wish List – Your Side

You've pulled together your product manager, pricing manager and someone from the legal department for this estimation and, after much wrangling, have prioritized your wish list of trades related to length of contract, price, volume, upgrades, installation and ongoing service.

Wish List Estimation: *Your Side*			
Rank	Item	Weight	Range
1	Length of contract	30%	3–1 Years
2	Price	25%	$300–250K per machine
3	Volume	15%	3–2 machines
4	Upgrades	15%	50% discount – free
5	Man hours you provide for installation	10%	100–150
6	Ongoing service	5%	8 hours x 5 days – 24 hours x 7 days

Prepare Wish List – The Other Side

With the help of the account manager who used to work for your competitor and your pricing manager, you've estimated the types of trades this company has looked for in the past and come up with the following educated guesses for its Wish List.

Wish List Estimation: *The Other Side*			
Rank	**Item**	**Weight**	**Range**
1	Price	40%	$300–250K per machine
2	Ongoing service	25%	24 hours x 7 days – 8 hours x 5 days
3	Upgrades	15%	Free – 75% discount
4	Length of contract	10%	1 year – ??
5	Volume	5%	2 machines – ??
6	Man hours you provide for installation	5%	200–100

Prepare CNA & Wish List Questions for Customer

You know exactly what the customer's CNA is and you've done a pretty good job of analyzing its positive and negative elements. Now in order to validate your assumptions about your customer's CNA, to learn how your customer sees its CNA and to educate the customer on the reality of their CNA, you prepare the following questions for them:

- Have you determined how much customization the two machines will need for installation?
- How will your facility be impacted during installation?
- Do you have a certain amount of time budgeted for installation?
- What are your expectations in terms of machine downtime?
- When the machine breaks down, how quickly do you expect service?
- How much staff retraining do you expect you'll need?
- Do you have a figure in mind for maintenance costs in the first year?

154

- Do you have figures in mind for costs in years two through four?
- How would you like to handle future upgrades?
- Do you complete TCO analyses or just compare acquisition price?

You also develop questions to validate the customer's Wish List items as follows:

- I understand you will be looking to negotiate price, service, upgrades, length of contract, volume and man hours to install. Is that right? Is there anything missing? Is there anything that should be deleted?
- What list item would you rank as your highest priority? That is, what should we focus on most? How about second, third, fourth, etc.?
- Do you have any specific targets you'd like to hit for each item?

Meet with Customer to Validate and Refine Assumptions

Now you send out an e-mail to the head buyer, the vice president of manufacturing, the vice president of finance and all the other people to whom you've been selling. You ask for 15 minutes of their time to better understand their needs for the upcoming negotiation. If they ask for them, you can send the questions in advance.

When you get together with each client representative, on the phone or in person, ask the easy Wish List questions first to get the ball rolling, then go on to the CNA questions. Bring someone else from your account team with you to record the customer's answers.

Having had meetings with your buying influences on several levels to validate your assumptions, you now feel that, even though the customers didn't answer all your questions, you were able to tighten up your estimations. You also feel that you succeeded in educating them on many aspects of their CNA as well as on many of the items to be agreed upon in the negotiation.

Design and Deliver Three MEOs

Start by asking yourself: What three problems am I solving, what risk-sharing alternatives am I offering or what creative partnerships are possible with this customer?

Your CNA analysis revealed two or three ways you solved this customer's needs better than their alternatives, so you create and name your MEOs in ways that describe each of these solutions. Use customer language that punches a point of value and exploits your strength. The MEOs take into account your interest in and priorities for length of contract, price and volume as well as the customer's needs and priorities for price, service and upgrades. All three offers are equal to you (you would accept any one of them), but very different to your customer.

Item	Option 1: Short-Term Relationship and Lower Price	Option 2: Long-Term Strategic Relationship	Option 3: A Middle Ground
Length	One year	Three years	Two years
Price	$295K per machine	$250K per machine	$275K per machine
Volume	One machine	Three machines	Two machines
Service	8 hours x 5 days	24 hours x 7 days	24 hours x 5 days
Upgrades	50% discount	Free	75% discount
Installation Support	100 hours	300 hours	200 hours

It's May 7th, a full week before the customer's due date, and you're ready to make a presentation. You invite the customer's head buyer, the vice president of manufacturing and the vice president of finance, and bring along product and technical support people from your side.

- **Open the presentation:** start by thanking the group for taking the time to answer your questions a few weeks earlier. Let attendees know that this went a long way toward helping you customize three different potential relationships.

- **State client's CNA:** Tell the group that you realize that if they don't choose you they will choose your nearest competitor, and admit that your competitor has a pretty good off-the-shelf solution as well as pretty good output.

Also note that during your earlier conversations, the buyer and the vice president of finance put a lot of emphasis on price, and that the vice president of manufacturing talked a lot about up-time, that is, the reliability of machines.

Now present the value proposition gap you found in your CNA analysis, specifically:

- *Your machines are priced higher in the short-term (year one).*
- *Your machines are X percent more reliable than your competitor's, resulting in higher output (manufacturing's concern) and less maintenance cost (buyer's and finance department's request).*
- *The combination of higher output and lower maintenance makes your machines cost less starting late in year one, then drop by Y percent in years two and three.*

- **Review the three MEO titles and briefly summarize the solution each MEO provides:** You tell them that based on their needs and the value proposition of your competitor, you've put together three different relationships (highlighted on a flipchart or in a PowerPoint® presentation).

- **Review the trades in each MEO:** You briefly overview some key trades in each offer, then give everyone a handout containing the details and go through them.

- **Rank the MEOs:** You ask everyone present to rank the three offers in terms of their preference.

- **Continue trading:** The client quickly agrees that the short-term option is the least preferable, but there's a lot of internal negotiation among them over which of the remaining options is better. It's obvious that neither is quite right. At this point, you begin trading to come up with one solution that fits their needs. They keep telling you that you're more expensive; you keep going back to total costs. They try to push you for concessions; you continue to trade using both wish lists.

In the end, you settle on this deal:

Final Agreement

Length: Three years

Price: $255K per machine

Volume: Three machines

Service: Five days x 24 hours

Upgrades: 25% discount

Installation Support: 300 hours

APPENDIX

Negotiation for Sales Effectiveness
Benchmarking Current and
Best Practice
A Report by the Strategic Account
Management Association and Think! Inc.

Negotiation for Sales Effectiveness
Benchmarking Current and Best Practice
A Report by the Strategic Account Management Association and Think! Inc.

Section

Section 1: Executive summary

There has been great emphasis on research related to initiatives such as goal setting, compensation, account management, sales strategy and sales process. In contrast, there has been almost no attention paid to negotiation. This inspired the Strategic Account Management Association (SAMA) and Think! Inc. to benchmark the current state of negotiation against other professional skills and practices in the selling and account managing fields. The purpose: to measure today's standard of negotiation and suggest how to raise that standard to best practice.

We believe that the state of negotiation today is one of unconscious incompetence. In other words, either we aren't aware of a hazard in front of us or we don't realize that the situation ahead is dangerous. A fable will illustrate the insights emerging from this survey.

A Grim Fairy Tale of Margin and Brand Equity Erosion

Once upon a time there was a negotiating marketplace where the sellers were comprised of huge multinational companies. These sellers were distributed throughout 25 industries. All the sellers had massive sales forces, many of which were the cream of the crop, from national and global account managers to the leadership. These salespeople and their leaders focused on the largest and most profitable customers for their companies.

Seller No. 1 noticed that the marketplace was being flooded by aggressive professional buyers. They demanded massive price discounts while simultaneously pushing hard for Seller No. 1 to provide valuable parts of its value proposition for free. To further complicate matters, the seller's competitors were prone to irrational behavior, giving in to buyers' demands and getting nothing in return. All the while, deals in the marketplace were becoming bigger, longer term, more strategic and fewer in numbers, making each one increasingly important. To combat this, the seller had a negotiation strategy/plan that featured:

- *Limited internal cross-functional agreement on how to combat what was happening in the negotiation marketplace*
- *Very little proactive planning to deal with the increasing irrational competitive behavior*
- *Almost no consistent planning for the bigger, longer term and more strategic deals*
- *Barely any consistent sales force practices or processes on how to negotiate with customers*
- *Almost no integration of selling and negotiating*
- *A tendency to accept customer demands for zero sum concessions*

Seller No. 1 looked at its peers and saw similar strategies. Recognizing that these strategies might be suboptimal, the seller reached out to traditional tactic-based negotiation training firms and put its sales team through negotiation training.

162

After training, almost everything stayed the same.

The seller considered its negotiation performance in the marketplace. Like most of its competitors, it determined it was between somewhat effective and effective as a negotiator.

That fable summarizes the research in this report. Internally, corporations have little to no proactive cross-functional agreement on what negotiation success might look like or how to accomplish it one negotiation at a time.

For the most part, negotiation is considered a set of soft skills made up of reactive verbal tactics. No wonder it remains an elective in professional sales development. This mistake should no longer be made given the amount of margin and brand equity that negotiation puts at risk. We in the negotiation industry have set our standards too low. Sales professionals are ill-equipped to stand up to the professional negotiators and purchasing officers, so it's natural for the marketplace to struggle with margin pressure. Our research finds that this trend can be easily reversed through redefining negotiation standards and setting new negotiation benchmarks consisting of:

Negotiation strategy best-practice standards

- Internal agreement on negotiation strategy, which maps where we want to go
- A common negotiation process and language that shows sales professionals how to get there
- Placing more decision-making power in the hands of dealmakers
- Completely integrated selling and negotiating processes

Negotiation process best-practice standards

- Regularly scheduled negotiation planning sessions
- An established, repeatable negotiation process
- Trading instead of conceding; never giving away something for nothing
- Internal support for the sales team through corporate-wide agreement on what is and is not negotiable, so the team can confidently move forward at the negotiation table

In essence, sales professionals, their leaders and negotiation providers must transform their approach to negotiation. Kurt Lewin, a pioneer of social psychology, said changing behavior consists of three phases:

1. Creating the motivation to change by unfreezing attitudes
2. Developing new attitudes and behaviors based on new information that shifts perspective
3. Integrating and stabilizing those changes

Consider this: If you have a large cube of ice but prefer a cone of ice, what do you do? You melt the ice to make it amenable to change (unfreeze). Then you mold the ice water into the shape you want (change). Finally, you solidify the new shape (refreeze).

This report explores each of these stages as they relate to establishing a new negotiation paradigm. However, success will happen only when we are motivated to change the way we think about negotiation and the results we expect from it.

Overview of the report

- There were 361 respondents
- Forty-seven percent were vice presidents or directors of sales, marketing or sales training
- Forty-six percent held positions such as strategic account manager, global account manager or national account manager
- Nearly half the companies had sales revenues between $3 billion and $6 billion
- Twenty-five industries were represented

About Think! Inc. and the Strategic Account Management Association (SAMA)

Think! Inc. is a high return-on-investment (ROI) consulting firm redefining the business-to-business negotiation training marketplace at both the strategic/ organizational effectiveness and tactical/skills level. At the strategic level, management needs only ask two questions: What happens to both sides if a deal does not happen, and what is likely to be included for both sides if a deal does happen? At the tactical level, participants need only know three key analytical concepts: the consequences of no agreement; anchor; and trade. For more information please visit www.e-thinkinc.com.

The Strategic Account Management Association (SAMA) is a knowledge-sharing organization devoted to developing, promoting and advancing the concept of customer-supplier collaboration through communities of practice. SAMA is dedicated to the professional development of the individuals and companies involved in the process of managing national, global and strategic customer relationships and to enabling members to create greater customer value and achieve competitive advantage accordingly. For more information please visit www.strategicaccounts. org.

Section 2: Demographics of the research

Summary

Our research explored an optimal balance of responses from sales management and line-level sales professionals within large- to medium-sized companies in terms of revenues and sales forces. These selling organizations, spanning 25 industries, focused on national, global and strategic account management.

Data

- Of the 361 respondents, 47 percent were vice presidents or directors of sales, marketing or sales training. Forty-six percent held positions such as strategic account manager, global account manager or national account manager. The rest were field-level managers and sales representatives.
- Nearly half had sales revenues between $3 billion and $6 billion.
- Twenty-five industries were represented. The largest was the chemical, petroleum and plastics industry. The second largest was business services, followed by electronic and electrical equipment, then transportation.
- More than half had 15,000 to 30,000 employees.
- Sales force size was divided equally between the ranges of 1,500 to 3,000 and 100 to 1,500.
- There was global representation with respondents from North, Central and South America, Asia/Pacific, Europe/United Kingdom and Middle East/ Africa, with the majority of respondents being from North America and Europe/United Kingdom.

Section 3: External market; customers and competitors

Summary

This section focuses on exogenous factors affecting corporate negotiation — the things out of our control. The marketplace is being flooded by professional buyers who are increasingly aggressive in demanding price discounts and giveaways. Deals are bigger, and there are fewer of them. Irrational competitive behavior is on the rise: Some competitors concede to buyers' demands regardless of how it may damage margins or brands. All of these factors point to the need for a new, systematic, long-term, organized approach to negotiation.

Data

- Ninety-two percent of respondents reported facing a higher number of professional buyers, such as procurement officers and senior sourcing executives, during sales negotiation. While sales professionals' core competence is selling and account management, buyers' core competence is negotiation. What's more, professional buyers are often aided by high-powered outside consultants who plan and execute negotiation strategy. Meanwhile, sellers know very little about how the professional procurement organizations function or are compensated. Contrary to what buyers say, they are at least as much concerned about total cost of ownership as they are about acquisition price.
- Additionally, 91 percent reported increasingly price-conscious customers. That's to be expected with the new breed of professional buyer.
- As a response to buyer pressure, 80 percent said they see mounting irrational

competitive behavior, such as competitors drastically lowering prices or giving away services. This happens because there's a lack of negotiation strategy, which drives irrational market behaviors and price and giveaway wars, ultimately lowering margins for everyone.

- Sixty percent said deals are becoming more commodity-like or somewhat commodity-like. With increasing pressure from professional buyers, we expect respondents to see even more commoditization pressure.
- An overwhelming 84 percent said customers are demanding more concessions.
- Eighty-nine percent reported that their customer relationships are becoming somewhat to very much longer term. Negotiation is much more important in a long-term than a short-term relationship. Consequently, it's critical to think more strategically about how negotiation plays out because it will impact both sides for a longer time.
- Ninety percent reported some kind of consolidation of their customer base. The result: Deals are becoming bigger, more strategic and more important for both sides. Again, negotiation plays an even more critical role. The relationship you negotiate is the relationship you live with.
- Eighty-five percent reported consolidations on the selling side. Fewer buyers and fewer sellers mean there are fewer, larger deals necessitating a more strategic negotiation approach.

Section 4: Internal negotiation — strategy alignment

Summary

Negotiation strategy should encompass internal, cross-functional alignment on what negotiation success looks like. That is, every department that touches negotiation – from legal to product management, from operations to marketing – would agree upon what constitutes successful negotiation outcomes. Negotiation process is how to get there one deal at a time.

Given the aggressiveness and irrationality in the market, we were interested to see how companies rise to meet today's negotiation challenges. Many people still define negotiation as a series of verbal tactics fired at buyers in the heat of battle. Regardless of one's definition, negotiation begins long before then. It begins even before the sales process.

Negotiation should begin with internal, cross-functional stakeholders creating agreement on negotiation "guardrails" and outcomes. Guardrails set the high and low boundaries for how much sales professionals can maneuver to close a deal. The boundaries establish the range for trading in and out of a deal. (Strategic negotiation is about far more than determining mere price for volume. It's about everything you have to offer that the competition doesn't, from length of contract to delivery and from follow-up to customer support and service. The list could go on and on because there are boundless creative ways to position the terms of the deal beyond volume and money.)

What we see from the research is that sales strategy is more internally aligned than negotiation strategy. Organizations have little formal agreement on where their collective negotiations are taking them, while their prospects' negotiation experts know precisely where they want the negotiation to go and how to get there. This fact coupled with irrationality in the market has the potential to push the marketplace toward margin disaster while decimating brand equity along the way.

Much as sales process drives revenue, negotiation controls margin. They occasionally cross over, but negotiation either enhances or detracts from the margin created during the sales campaign. However, there is no plan for margin protection or goals for margin growth without internal, cross-functional alignment on negotiation strategy.

Negotiation also represents the brand. Every negotiation sends a message to customers, competitors and sales forces. You can't claim you're the value leader when everyone knows that at the final hour your prices will sink faster than the Titanic. How you negotiate is either a deposit or withdrawal from your brand equity. Giving away value tarnishes brand perception and signals competitors to do the same, triggering irrational competitive behavior that can obliterate everyone's margins.

In essence, after reviewing this research and studying almost 20,000 deals over the past 10 years in 46 countries, there is a shocking lack of negotiation strategy. In most cases, by default, negotiation strategy is defined by negotiation tactics. In contrast, the most successful negotiators use negotiation strategy to drive tactics.

Data

- Companies were three times more likely to have a sales strategy than a negotiation strategy. More specifically, 83 percent of respondents said they have no negotiation strategy or merely an implied one. If we define strategy and process as where we want to go and how we want to get there, it's no wonder there's more irrational competitive behavior.
- Eighty-one percent reported moderate-, high- or extremely high-level internal negotiation, which is just as important as external customer negotiation. Without internal alignment on strategy (negotiation guardrails and desired outcomes), there's confusion and internal silo competition. Sales strategy has sellers bringing solutions and total value propositions to the marketplace, yet internally they are required to negotiate this solution with separate silos and separate profit and loss statements.
- There is not a high level of collaboration between sales and other cross-functional departments, reported 55 percent. But collaboration is so critical to intelligent negotiation strategy that this percentage should be as high as 70 or 80 percent.

In a number of areas C-suite executives and street-level sales professionals had significantly differing responses:

- Executives were 46 percent more likely than salespeople to believe that their firms were extremely proactive in managing negotiations, while salespeople were 43 percent more likely to believe that their firms were extremely reactive.
- Executives were 36 percent more likely to believe that their negotiation and sales processes were integrated.
- Executives were 77 percent more likely to view their decision-making authority as highly centralized, while salespeople were 71 percent more likely to view it as somewhat or highly decentralized.

The implication is there is a disconnect between street-level and executive management caused by the absence of negotiation strategy and process. This is exacerbated by the absence of internal, cross-functional alignment. This disconnect can not only cause marketplace confusion, it can create internal strife.

- Negotiation decision-making is becoming more centralized, reported 71 percent.

Here are the benefits of centralized decision-making: It provides more control over brand equity; prevents sales professionals from sending mixed messages about the value proposition; and decreases variance in pricing. Here are the dangers: Waiting for a centralized authority to approve a deal often grinds negotiation to a halt, and, what's more, centralized negotiation is very customer unfriendly, leaves no room for creativity and puts salespeople and account managers in the unenviable position of not being empowered to make decisions.

The other school of negotiation strategy is one of decentralization—that is, to let those closest to the deals make real-time negotiation decisions because "they know best." The benefits of this approach are faster, more customer-friendly and creative deals. The dangers are that sometimes those deals are a little too creative, hurting margins and brand with too much variance and zero-based decisions.

There is a new school of thought, however, that accentuates the benefits of centralized negotiation authority while diminishing the drawbacks. It's called radically centralized strategy with radically decentralized execution, and it is structured around the concept of guardrails we discussed in Section 3. Recently, we met with 26 cross-functional managers who somehow touched internal and external negotiation. This group approved high and low ranges on nearly 70 aspects of its organizations' value propositions. These 70 potential trades were put directly in the hands of salespeople. The net effect has been better, faster decisions at the market level, tightened variance on negotiation exceptions and an empowered sales force.

Section 5: External negotiation – tactics alignment

Summary

We know from the previous two sections that customers are becoming more aggressive and demanding more price decreases and zero-sum concessions (i.e., expecting something for nothing). Competitors behave irrationally by giving away portions of their value proposition. Respondents have little formal internal alignment on negotiation strategy. Now, we see how all that impacts external tactics. There is very little formal planning for negotiation, almost no systematic process for executing that plan, sales and negotiation are rarely integrated, we are rarely trading for customer demands and have little plan to deal with competitor irrationality.

Data

- Companies were three times more likely to have a sales process than a negotiation process. More specifically, 85 percent of respondents said they have no negotiation process or merely an implied one. If we define strategy and process as where we want to go and how we want to get there, it's no wonder there's more irrational competitive behavior.
- Only nine percent of respondents said they have a well-defined strategy to respond to competitive behaviors like drastically lowering prices or giving away services.
- Only 11 percent reported that their organizations are extremely proactive in negotiation.
- Conversely, 89 percent reported they are not extremely proactive in negotiation. This is shocking considering that when they reach the negotiation table, they're going head to head with professional negotiators on fewer, bigger, longer term and more strategic deals.
- Only five percent rated their capability in customer negotiation as highly effective.
- Sixty-two percent reported that their negotiation process is not integrated with their sales process or that both are nonexistent. An integral part of resolving complex negotiation problems is thinking about negotiations much earlier in the sales cycle and ultimately erasing the line between selling and negotiation. After all, you negotiate what you sell.
- In the face of increased demands for concessions, respondents are missing a powerful opportunity to build margins by trading – i.e., getting something in return for anything you give. Trading is essentially what pays for the deal: the total terms of the solution. Unfortunately, 79 percent said they occasionally or do not effectively trade for customer demands. They're accustomed to giving customers something for nothing. This erodes credibility and brand equity. By giving away value, sales professionals tell customers that the original price was a lie.

Consider one of our clients, a small components manufacturer that regularly sold products to a computer giant that hired procurement consultants to do its deals. Year after year, the manufacturer rolled over every time the consultants asked for a giveaway. We taught our client to stop giving away value and start asking for something of value in return. The seller-buyer relationship subsequently improved; the manufacturer had gained the computer giant's respect and greater trust.

Section 6: Account-specific strategy and tactics

Summary

Negotiation strategy comes in many shapes and sizes. Smaller firms may have one strategy for their company. Other firms have strategies around products or regions of the world. The most explicit negotiation strategies are those written for specific national or global accounts. Given the strategic importance of these accounts, we extracted a subset of data on negotiation strategy and process related to the biggest and most profitable national and global organizations. The results were surprising. There was still a high degree of reactive tactics and zero-sum concessions regardless of the size or importance of the customer.

Data

- Sixty-six percent of respondents were either in management or the field level for national or global customer management teams. These teams should be the standard-bearers for any corporate sales force, and we were disappointed with their level of sophistication regarding negotiation.
- While 63 percent said they had account-specific sales strategies, only 16 percent had account-specific negotiation strategies.
- While 42 percent reported that they had account-specific sales processes in place, only 15 percent said they had account-specific negotiation processes.
- The percentage who had no account-specific negotiation strategy or process was the same as the general survey: 83 percent. What this tells us is that regardless of the size or importance of the customer, managers of the largest and most profitable accounts still are not using a proactive negotiation strategy or process. But professional buyers never come to the negotiation table without it.

Section 7: New standards

Summary

The results of this survey are a battle cry to overcome commoditization and uphold genuine value. We must completely redefine everything we know about negotiation and demand a new standard.

The marketplace is flooded with aggressive, professional buyers, competitors are behaving more irrationally and giving away value, and there are fewer opportunities to make deals. Plus, the deals that are made are longer term. In the face of all this, sellers report reasonable sophistication on sales strategy and process as well as account-specific sales strategy and process. But they have virtually no negotiation strategy and process.

Strategy is defined as where we want to go, and process is defined as how we will get there one deal at a time. Without strategy and process, no less than one embraced internally and cross-functionally aligned across an organization, it's no wonder today's state of negotiation is so dismal.

It's so dismal, in fact, even traditional training doesn't help. Consider this: In the past two years about 50 percent of respondents have attended traditional negotiation skills training classes, which focus on long lists of tactics and counter-responses. At first glance, we were surprised that more organizations aren't pursuing negotiation training for their sales professionals. But the results point to why it isn't more sought after: Traditional negotiation training just doesn't work. Of the roughly 50 percent that pursued traditional negotiation skills training, 6.8 percent (only 1.8 percent higher than the entire pool of respondents) rated themselves afterward as highly effective negotiators. Reports on their level of proactive planning and trading versus conceding also stayed almost flat.

Here's why: Negotiation is still perceived as a soft skill – tactics and verbal sparring – that is the domain of sales professionals. Strategic negotiation is far bigger. It encompasses every department that touches sales. Well before any sales professional reaches the negotiation table, no less makes that first sales call, there must be internal agreement on where negotiation should go (strategy) and how sales professionals will get there (process). On a broader level, there should be strategy and process built around responding to key competitors and key customers. One of the problems with traditional negotiation training is that many trainers have incorrectly diagnosed negotiation problems as tactical and therefore prescribed incorrect solutions. From watching almost 20,000 business negotiations over 10 years in 46 countries, we know that the diagnosis and prescription for negotiation is more strategic than tactical. Good strategies drive good tactics. In fact, world-class dealmakers need only to be able to answer two questions to effectively "blueprint" a deal and anticipate what is likely to occur tactically by competitors and customers.

1. What are the consequences to both sides in the event of no agreement (i.e., the consequences of no agreement, also known as CNA)?
2. What are the likely terms in the event an agreement is reached (i.e., trades)?

Answering these two questions effectively blueprints a business negotiation, populating the two squares and circles in the graphic below. Virtually every tactical thing that occurs in a negotiation is governed by this blueprint data. The problem in negotiation is not that we need more training on how to respond but rather that we need more data on the blueprint to effectively respond.

Fortunately most corporations are well-acquainted with the effectiveness of strategy and process, and many consider it key to their sales success. According to CSO Insights' 13th annual survey of sales performance optimization, 85 percent of respondents that have a formal sales process report that it has positively impacted sales performance.[1]

It would follow, then, that integrating sales and negotiation strategy and process would create even more impressive outcomes. And it has. Consider that organizations have reported a 200-percent ROI within six months of:[2]

- Attaining internal agreement on where they want to go in negotiation (negotiation strategy)
- Establishing a common negotiation process and language that shows sales professionals how to get there
- Building internal support for the sales team through corporate-wide agreement on what is and is not negotiable so the team can confidently move forward at the negotiation table
- Placing more decision-making power in the hands of dealmakers
- Completely integrating selling and negotiating processes
- Regularly scheduling negotiation planning sessions
- Developing a repeatable negotiation process
- Deciding always to trade and never concede or give something away for nothing

Those organizations raised their standards for negotiation and achieved impressive outcomes. This demonstrates tremendous room for growth for firms willing to redefine how they approach negotiation.[3]

Section 8: Demonstrating ROI

As mentioned earlier, Kurt Lewin's first phase for changing behavior is "creating the motivation to change by unfreezing attitudes." From an executive perspective, a high ROI, driven by significant improvements to the organization's profits, is often the motivation to unfreeze attitudes. A mathematical approach to looking at profit contribution from a salesperson or sales team is as follows:

$$Annual\ Profit = \frac{\#\ Deals\ in\ Pipeline \times \$\ Avg\ Deal\ Size \times Close\ Rate\ \% \times Avg\ Deal\ Gross\ Margin\ \%}{Avg\ Sales\ Cycle\ Length\ (months)}$$

A technical definition of ROI is the monetary benefits derived from spending money on developing or revising a system. Mathematically, this can be shown as:

$$ROI = \frac{Incremental\ Profits}{Incremental\ Expenses}$$

Incremental expenses in this instance can be defined as money paid to training/consulting firms for workshops, plus salaries for internal employees involved with training, as well as participants' travel and lodging expenses.

We previously referenced organizations that have reported a 200-percent ROI within six months. Many executives see such an ROI and are justifiably concerned whether it is from financial parlor tricks. We encourage you to plug your own numbers into a hypothetical example to see what improvements you would need to make to achieve your desired ROI.

Let's say a hypothetical sales representative has $1 million in annual sales. She has pursued 40 deals with a 50 percent close rate – i.e., she has closed 20 deals at $50,000 apiece. Assuming a gross margin of 20 percent on each deal, this sales professional has contributed $200,000 of annual gross profit.

$$Annual\ Profit = \$200K = \frac{20\ Deals \times \$50K\ Avg\ Deal \times 50\%\ Close\ Rate \times 20\%\ Avg\ Deal\ Margin}{6\ month\ Avg\ Sales\ Cycle\ Length}$$

When integrating sales and negotiation strategy and process, a firm might set metrics for success as follows:

- Eliminate 10 percent of its deals through better qualification
- Increase the average deal size by 10 percent and the average deal gross margin by 10 percent through always trading and never conceding
- Improve the close rate by five percent (e.g., increasing it from 50 percent to 55 percent)
- Decrease the sales cycle length by five percent

By hitting those metrics, the organization would achieve a 25 percent increase in overall profit (or $50,000 for the year), calculated as follows:

$$Annual\ Profit = \$250K = \frac{18\ Deals \times \$55K\ Avg\ Deal \times 55\%\ Close\ Rate \times 22\%\ Avg\ Deal\ Margin}{5\frac{3}{4}\ month\ Avg\ Sales\ Cycle\ Length}$$

For the first 12 months, if the total incremental expenses were $5,000 per person for the training, and assuming the $50,000 total incremental profit per person above, then the ROI for training would be 1,000 percent for the first year.

Actual mileage may vary, but we encourage you to follow the math to see if your attitudes should unfreeze based on the potential ROI in your organization.

Endnotes:

[1] Jim Dickie and Barry Trailer, "Sales Performance Optimization: 2007 Survey Results and Analysis," CSO Insights, 2007, www.csoinsights.com.

[2] Return-on-investment case studies for Ryder System Inc., D&B, SkillSoft PLC and Livingston International Inc., Think! Inc, www.e-thinkinc.com.

[3] For additional reading:

Danny Ertl, "Turning Negotiation into a Corporate Capability," Harvard Business Review, May-June 1999, reprint #99304, www.hbr.com.

Brian Dietmeyer, "A Blueprint for Effective Negotiation," Harvard Management Update, July 2004, reprint #U0407B, http://harvardbusinessonline.hbsp.harvard.edu.

Participant comments

Participants in this survey were asked to rate the level of negotiation effectiveness at their companies and/or their sales or account management programs, and offers reasons why. Their answers fill the following pages.

Question: Overall, how would you rate your own company's capabilities and performance in customer negotiations and why?

Rating:

1) highly effective
2) effective
3) somewhat effective
4) not effective

Comments from companies and/or programs rated <u>highly effective</u> in negotiating with customers

- We have a high level of internal collaboration and alignment during the negotiation process.
- We have a team that is dedicated to customer negotiations.
- Our program is based on results and the use of a highly effective process.
- Negotiating is an integral part of our business.
- We almost always have the knowledge of the customers and drivers to ensure that we know what value they attach to each point and negotiate effectively.
- The negotiators are highly skilled and competent. Even though there may be room for improvements in terms of strategic planning of negotiations, the whole set up is very competent.
- Our senior staff is focused on making money, therefore we negotiate.
- We achieve the same results with less bureaucracy and administrative work.

Comments from companies and/or programs rated <u>effective</u> in negotiating with customers

- Everyone on our sales team tries to show value when negotiating with accounts, especially in the wake of rising prices.
- We use input from sales, legal and finance during negotiations. While we don't have a formal, written sales/negotiations process, we consistently achieve our targets — revenue and profit.
- We have developed a defined sales process and modified the steps according to the sales complexity involved, e.g., selling a mom & pop shops as opposed to selling to a large corporate office. In so doing we have grown sales to double-digit growth in an industry that is growing 1-3% per year.
- We are effective because there is an interaction and proactivity among the company in different departments in order to get any business. Of course there is much to be improved.

- We identify the appropriate stakeholders, understand what they value and determine a strategy that brings value to the buying and selling organization in a systematic approach.
- Customers seldom walk away from the negotiation table nor do we, whilst achieving an acceptable hit rate.
- There is great deal of variability between individuals and units. We know what to do, we want to do the right things, but we don't always make the time to do it right.
- Due to the number of processes, we take longer than our competition to react. We are starting to be proactive to pre-sell our "trades" so that we are in a position to negotiate on our own, showing empowerment.
- We focus, train and integrate negotiating into our account planning process. Our ultimate goal is to develop more collaborative relationships, focus on value rather than price. We are moving away from competitive negotiations where possible.
- We have an internal team that has been effective in securing business when we are in competitive negotiations. I would estimate a 90 percent success rate. We have a growing market share in the segment of the market where pricing concessions are being made. The majority of our business is done at a prescribed industry rate.
- We plan our negotiations approach and strategy taking into consideration information obtained about the customer's thought process, prioritized needs, concerns and issues and respond to these accordingly during the negotiations.
- We do our best not to react to an irrational or unprofitable request. In some cases though, if the opportunity is large enough, then we are more likely to reduce margins without receiving anything in return. This is due to the fact that we have a decentralized sales force across 16 different plants.
- We provide sales training to our sales reps depending on level in the organization (basic-, versatile-, target account-sales). Although negotiation training is not well addressed, we work in teams, and the mix of selling and negotiating skills within teams makes us an effective party in negotiations.
- We have corporate standards, processes and tool boxes in place, conduct gap assessments and develop skills to close gaps at the market level according to the accounts' levels of sophistication. Our established customer relationships, combined with brand/logistics power allow for effective negotiations, even though a firm process does not exist.
- My company has a defined process for customer negotiations as well as a cross functional team that participates in strategy development for negotiations.
- We generally achieve the targets that we set during our planning sessions. Acceptable alternatives are considered during these sessions, and we are usually able to work with our customers to reach an outcome that is good for both of us.

- There is a documented sales process in place with a small element of the process being negotiation. We are getting more effective at negotiating via following the process.
- We have a global sales force and not all members are sophisticated negotiators. We are working to create a sales force with consistent high-level negotiation skills.
- We have a strong overall account relationship, and delivering value can make the negotiation process easier.
- We specifically target clients that have specific needs or requirements. Primarily, we have segmented the market based on commodity, fully explored the needs and requirements of the market, fully explored what our competitors are providing and created value-added service to differentiate our brand.
- Being specialty in nature, our products give us some leverage in negotiation where other commodity-type products have none. We are therefore prone to ask and expect more out of negotiation than others.
- We speak in business terms at the initial meeting, linking the initiative as tightly as possible to the organization's business direction. We encourage a lot of questions and are prepared to answer them well. This drives executive alignment and improves the likelihood that the initiative gets off on the right foot.
- We are able to adapt ourselves to the customer demands and to be somewhat creative in negotiation.
- We can quickly pull together the 5-6 key stakeholders and make quick decisions. We have had a high rate of contract renewals with minimal negative disruption in the relationship.
- We are able to put together a team at the beginning of the negotiation process and have been able to get the decision we need to make successful deals that senior management always approves of, because there is always someone from senior mgmt on the team.

Comments from companies and/or programs rated <u>somewhat effective</u> in negotiating with customers

- It depends on the customer. Some large clients have a structured process that we follow. We do well with large clients who focus on win/win agreements.
- Too many layers of management make the process complicated. There should be 'empowerment' give to all levels.
- We usually go in with a mix of fear and greed, instead of looking for mutually acceptable long-term agreements.
- Negotiation is still too much of an individual sales person skill and not a corporate process. We are currently addressing this. We are aware there is space for improvement and a clear demand for it.
- Although we try to be proactive in preparing for negotiations, hostile moves

by competitors for short term gains actually result in my company not being successful in the negotiations.

- We are not stopping all of the price erosion on our products. We are walking away more and doing it sooner in the process. We decide what we can and can't win sooner in the process than we used to.

- There is a lack of experience by senior management within our specific industry. New management has just been put in place and are inexperienced with the company's products and market trends at present.

- The goals of a strategic account are not always the goals of the management of core business units and hinder the efforts to have a total approach to the customer and sharing in risk and reward.

- Because we are decentralized, we are unable to leverage enterprise-wide solutions for our customers. We are not empowered to make these decisions on behalf of the individual business units; we have to gain their buy-in, which is time consuming.

- Most negotiations are reactive, whereby the sales rep must submit a proposal on behalf of the customer to obtain approval from the business case committee.

- We have a defined preferred provider pricing strategy and internal sign off processes. However, it could be better communicated internally, and our value proposition around value over price better defined and understood.

- The effectiveness of the negotiations is primarily due to the experience level of the individual rep, and across-the-board strategy or expected results are left up to the individual business units that cover the accounts.

- The intent and objectives at the senior management level are certainly to improve our skills in terms of customer relationships: having the right people in the right roles with the right skills and the right tools. Unfortunately, the sales force is being inundated with training sessions, and administrative and sales processes that are highly time-consuming thereby are taking away precious time, time that we need to work with our customers to understand their future business needs and as such, work more proactively and strategically.

- Our global locations act independently and do not collaborate for the greater good and to provide the best proposal. Some regions, like Europe, do a better job with negotiations than other regions. We believe we are not effectively demonstrating the value our services will deliver to our clients, and hence, we are not fully realizing our pricing potential and optimizing our profitability. Too easily we get bogged down in price/service negotiations.

- We negotiate price internally, not externally with the customer. We have a centralized pricing organization that sales typically negotiates with. It's typically after a negotiation with the price team that the sales rep goes back and negotiates with the customer.

- "Politically correct" decisions are often taken by senior management to preserve the relationship rather than the margin. These decisions are intended to avoid conflicts and relationship issues. We often give discounts to customers who do not live up to their end of the deal, i.e. they do not purchase the volumes promised, or we do not get unfettered access to their scientists.

- Due to the fact that we are a small nimble company, we have the ability to meet the customers' demands without creating turmoil in the industry. In addition, due to our cost competitiveness, we are in a good position more times than not.

- We are in an industry that regularly has to negotiate contracts, and the differences are usually somewhat insignificant. On the contracts that do require major negotiations, we have a fair amount of success having the contract to our benefit.

- Although we do not have a written process or strategy for negotiations in place, we are highly centralized in our decision-making authority for negotiating with the customer in our organization. Also, even with our reactive process for negotiations, the results that have been achieved are satisfactory.

- There is a disconnect between the sales process and actual contract negotiation process, limiting ability to effectively negotiate. Boundaries for sales professionals could be better established in order to make the process more efficient.

- For strategic accounts and opportunities, we ultimately pull together the right people and go through a process to develop a proposal or response. We can be effective, but it takes significant time and effort to get the results. A disciplined process would help to reduce response time and effort while increasing our effectiveness.

- We are not on same page many times within the organization. We offer too little. Then, when customer is contemplating switching, we make concessions many times too late. We don't allow sales to have parameters to negotiate, and if we need to go outside of the parameters, then we go to next level and get approval.

- When senior management decides that a customer is worthwhile or suits our purpose, then there is an increased presence, and resources are tied to it. Otherwise it becomes a struggle to gain internal buy-in.

- The negotiation skills of our account managers and their direct superiors who have direct responsibility on their accounts are not in place. They easily give up and give excuses that they can't reach the decision-makers (at the customer) who are in top management. To them, maintaining a good relationship means giving away things to customers and entertaining customers. We tried to change this paradigm, but it takes time, especially for older employees.

- Because our reps do not have good negotiating skills, they tend to try to please the customer without understanding the negotiation process. This leads to concessions and poor long-term profit performance. We also do little investigation into the customers' corporate needs to meet their objectives on our terms instead of theirs.

- We are very "siloed" as an organization, and it is very difficult to negotiate an agreement while maintaining the best interests of every individual operating group of our corporation.
- The negotiations always start on the customer's demand. We don't have a consistent process for the preparation of negotiations.
- With our larger clients we work very hard on our negotiations; however, they are more reactive than proactive. With the medium or smaller clients, we may not start with a strategy, and then when it grows, we may not have the best terms or strategy. We need to integrate our negotiations more clearly into our sales process.
- Our company is very good managing in RFPs and great with overall customer service. However, we have no formal way that we negotiate. We get business due to our size, scope and capacity in all markets.
- We lack strategic negotiation skills at most levels throughout the company and 'hero disease' is often invoked. We treat negotiations individually, failing to manage all negotiations across one strategy and/or fail to comprehend the impacts of one to another.
- Due to lack of scheduling and preparation, we generally have a poor vision of the key decision-makers and drivers. Thus we too often fail in making a differentiating and correctly targeted proposal. We then have to adjust our proposal as a reaction to our competitors or customer comments.
- Performance is based on a number of individuals whose skills vary. Performance ranges from highly effective to not effective. Thus, overall as an organization I would say we are somewhat effective.
- While we seem to win many negotiations, those wins are not crisp. Our competitors seem to lack in their negotiating ability, so refined skill and execution on our part could improve our capture ratios.

Comments from companies and/or programs rated <u>not effective</u> in negotiations with customers

- Our company has gone through numerous management changes at the CEO to the Director level. The National Account Program recently stabilized and has commitment from current management team, but many pieces, i.e. systems, training, marketing etc., need revamping to better serve the customer and build a competitive edge.
- We are giving a whole lot of value for free because of the threat to lose what we've got right now.
- Business is conducted on a day-to-day basis. Processes are drawn up but have neither been communicated, nor is there a desire to use them. Negotiations are conducted in a very individual manner.
- The market has changed dramatically over the past 12 months. We have had limited exposure to negotiations in the past. Strategies are in their infancy, and training has been limited.

- We lack an effective costing model which, in turn, compromises the pricing, which then makes negotiation less effective.
- We allow situations to become explosive before we react. By the time we begin to address the issue, it is seldom viable to resolve.
- Our Sales process is reactive in nature. We do not have a clear, defined sales process or negotiation process. A sales revenue goal is given to the sales VP, and they pass down their expectations to their sales managers.
- We are a very transactional sales organization built on a 100 percent commission structure with a lot of mavericks in the sales force. We also use the Sandler sales process, which fundamentally says that if you follow that process, there should be no need for negotiations.
- Ostensibly, we do not have a process, and negotiations are ad hoc depending on the rep and his or her influencing skills, credibility, etc.
- We have only begun to encounter procurement specialists in our negotiations over the past two years, leading to industry-specific experiences that have not been common to the majority of the company's US sales and management team.
- Negotiation is left to the ability of the account manager who may not be very effective or may not have the knowledge of what's possible or the contacts internally to gain agreement on negotiation points.
- We're in a rush (a 30-day mentality) to get the business, so we tend to give in to customer demands versus negotiate a win/win situation. Management is often too impatient to work through a negotiation process. They take the deal and move on regardless of the fact that we're impacting future business dealings with the customer by demonstrating that we'll quickly and easily relent to their demands when put under pressure (especially if there is a danger of not securing the business in our timeframe, i.e. quarter-end or year-end).
- The ability of people to understand how to use the tradeables we have as an organization and get something in return for trading something is negligible.
- Because we continue to see price erode, which tells me that part of our problem is in negotiating, We tend to either concede way too much and end up with a one-sided contract, or we fail to concede enough and lose the opportunity.

About the Author

Brian Dietmeyer is president, chief executive officer and co-counder of Think! Inc., a global strategic negotiation consultancy. Together with co-founder and business partner Dr. Max Bazerman, Dietmeyer customizes high ROI negotiation solutions, from custom training workshops to complex organization-wide initiatives, for companies in the business-to-business market. Before Think!, Dietmeyer served as

Brian Dietmeyer

vice president of national account sales for Marriott International, his most recent position during his 17-year tenure with the company. Earlier in his career, Dietmeyer was an ironworker laborer, a dump truck driver and an auto mechanic; none of those skills is current.

Dietmeyer received an undergraduate degree from De Paul University and an MBA from the J.L. Kellogg Graduate School of Management at Northwestern University.

Dietmeyer is a sought-after speaker and columnist, and author of the book *Strategic Negotiation*. He has served on the board of the Strategic Account Management Association (SAMA) and Chaired the MPI Adult Education Research Foundation. In his spare time Dietmeyer serves on the board of an at risk youth theatre company (Free Street Theatre) and donates time to Native American causes (American Indian Center). Dietmeyer is a native of Chicago, Illinois, USA.